From zero to 100 in six months

Dr Janne Ohtonen

Author: Dr Janne Ohtonen

Book cover by Dr Janne Ohtonen, Miika J. Norvanto

Publisher: IngramSpark

Language inspector: Grammarly; translated from Finnish by DeepL

1st English edition in 2024

ISBN 978-952-65401-0-8 (Book)

ISBN 978-952-65401-1-5 (EPUB)

ISBN 978-952-68055-9-7 (PDF)

A practical guide for you and me

So that both you and I can realize the best possible version of ourselves.

Table of contents

INTRODUCTION

We Finns are called direct, so let's put it so: *losers make excuses, while winners find ways to produce results regardless of their circumstances*! Often, our excuses sound so good that we don't get on with the task at hand.

What are some things you know are necessary or would like to promote but haven't started? We all have them. How can you test whether your favorite things are natural obstacles to getting things done?

Ask yourself: "Is there anyone else in this world who could have the same reasons for not doing this thing but has managed to do it anyway?"

"The first and greatest victory is to conquer yourself."
- Plato

If you are honest with yourself, you will almost certainly have to admit that thousands of others in the world have had it even worse but have still managed to do something great with their lives. For example, England has a dance club for people without functioning legs. It would be easy for me to say that I can never dance again because I'm in a wheelchair. However, these people have not let their disability stop them; they have developed their way of dancing together, all sitting in their wheelchairs. The hobby has proved to be so much fun that many people who can walk have joined them. In the same way that these people in this example have been able to turn a problematic obstacle into a strength, you can, too! *This book will give you motivation and practical exercises for achieving your goals* - not just one day, but soon, maybe even within six months. This book aims to empower you to believe in your ability to achieve great things and give you a concrete action plan for achieving your goals. The book also contains many practical exercises to use as a workbook on your own or with others.

So why bother with the extra effort, as you have a lot on your plate? Of course, today's world, based on a demanding economy, puts pressure on us to do more and do it more efficiently:

- **Inflation** means that more and more money is needed to maintain the same standard of living. Many of us also want more and more than we already have.

- Workplaces are constantly making things more **efficient**, which requires more to be done in the same amount of time. But because of this efficiency, work demands more and more of our time.

- Children's **education** has increasingly become the responsibility of parents. This requires time and concentration from children and parents and takes away from shared leisure and fun.

- TV, Netflix, Disney+, and other **entertainment** industries demand our time to consume the content.

- Increasing **illnesses**, sleep problems, and other health problems are taking more and more of our time to exercise and take care of our health.

- In addition to time and attention, **social media** increasingly requires us to invest more in ourselves. We're constantly competing with other piggy banks, fancy dinners, and spectacular holidays, not to mention other appearance and dress standards.

Today's #*demandeconomy* has taken away the ability to just sit at home on the couch and watch *The Voice* all night. Suppose you don't keep up with the demand economy; you risk being left out because you don't seem successful enough at work, home, or in your free time. Ever-increasing demands are demanding more and more of us, and that's why so many people end up in debt and burnout because the vicious circle of demand never stops! If you still take the time to use social media after reading this book, please share your experiences and insights on how the *#demandeconomy* has affected your life and the lives of those around you. In the past, we were content to make a living and care for our families. In the 1970s, family life was still seen as the most essential. Still, in the 1980s, family-centeredness was replaced by a relentless pursuit of profit, both in the workplace and in our personal lives. This eventually led to the recession of the early 1990s, which destroyed the lives of thousands of people (including my father). Not much was learned from that either, as the 2000s saw the so-called IT bubble*, and the 2010s saw the housing bubble (thanks to the banks' greed!). Now, in the 2020s, we will probably pop the human bubble, as a large part of the population will no longer be able to meet the demands of a demand economy and unexpected things such as the coronavirus, famine, tsunamis, volcanic eruptions in Iceland, floods and other natural disasters will devastate the world - not to mention the war in Ukraine and elsewhere with their long-term effects.

But every life-changing and world-changing event has its potential. We need to keep a cool head, manage the risk, and ensure that we don't get caught up in any unnecessary nonsense and don't miss out on the opportunities created by change. Having lived overseas for a long time, one Finnish folk trait has become apparent to me: some people think that one man's success is another man's loss. However, in every situation, there is always a group of people who lose and another group who gain, and the success of one is not necessarily taken away from the other. So, we all inevitably have two choices, and we can choose which of the following groups we want to belong to:

---

* The IT bubble of the 21st century was triggered from the mid 1990s onwards by the rapid spread of the Internet and new communication technologies, and the unrealistic economic expectations of the new services they enabled.

1. **People who can adapt to change and cope in all situations find ways to deliver results**. Circumstances turn into an opportunity for them, not a loss. They know how to change their thinking and work to best suit the circumstances.

2. **People who cannot adapt to changing circumstances will be left behind and likely suffer**. They will be victimized and lose their job, their spouse, or something else essential and not know what they can do. They also let other people's behavior (e.g., betrayal, property crime, vandalism) break them down internally and not just externally.

Some followers of Jesus have said that persecutors can break their bodies but not their spirits. This is a winning attitude because we cannot always prevent something or someone from breaking our bodies, possessions, circumstances, world, or image of the world around us. Indeed, my mentor, Anthony Robbins, has excellent advice: *we can't always choose what happens to us, but we can always choose how we deal with it*. Suppose you want to read exciting books that prove this statement true, for example. In that case, Viktor E. Frankl has written about German concentration camps, and a Chinese pastor known as Brother Heavenly/Brother Yun has written about the persecution of Christians in China. Both authors put the challenges of our own lives on a new scale. For us, the currency crisis of the 2020s and the war in Ukraine have significantly impacted many people's lives across Europe, forcing us to rethink things and our values.

So why bother getting up off your sofa and making the extra effort? Of course, you don't always have to be there to overcome the difficulties because there can also be treasure at the rainbow's end. People who make an effort to add value, grow their skills, and develop themselves will also reap greater rewards than those who find the call of the sofa irresistible:

- The top 1% earn 13% of all wages, and the top 10% earn 40% of all wages. That leaves 47% of salaries to be shared between the remaining 89%!

- ◆ Just under 10% of students receive the highest grade in each subject, the Laudatur (L).

- ◆ On average, around 10% of university applicants are accepted (in early 2020, in Finland, 13,821 university applicants were accepted, and 1,335 were admitted).

- ◆ Just over 10% of alcohol consumers drink around half of all alcohol consumed. It's not necessarily a statistic you want to be at the top of for your health.

- ◆ The top 10% of the rich own around 80% of all shares.

- ◆ Only 20% of women live to 100 and 95% of men to 95.

What if you could focus on what moves you towards the life and results you want? What opportunities would that open for you? How would it affect your happiness? Write your thoughts in the box below (and continue on another piece of paper if necessary):

Many people think that a passive life, lying on the couch and taking it easy, will bring happiness, but it's usually the opposite. People are creatures of meaning and purpose; the more they see meaning in themselves and their lives, the happier they are. This, in turn, comes through purposeful and satisfying activity. Yet, it often seems complicated to get oneself moving. Yet it's worth it and not so hard after all, when you know what to focus on and the steps that will lead you to your goal sustainably. Forget instant diets, getting rich in a few months without a job, a young lover from Nigeria, abdominal muscles without moving, and other similar scam programs; none of them work or produce the results you want. Sustainable experiences and results bring both satisfaction along the way and sustainable development as a human being.

Of course, most of us want to get rich, lose weight, build up our abs, learn more things, and add value to others. Many of us even know what to do to achieve these things, or at least what we need to start doing to make progress. But when it comes to getting things done, the timeline is all too often that famous old *someday* that never comes. Thus, from time to time, most of us, myself included, are more effective in making excuses for doing something later than spending at least some of the same amount of time making progress on what we want to do! So, this book is for people who don't want to live their lives in that *one-day* timeline but are willing to take a step forward, however small. By following the advice in this book, you can achieve your long-term goals and dreams faster and more permanently. You don't necessarily have to work hard to achieve significant results but rather focus on the essentials.

I had always postponed sport on the pretext that I didn't have time for it because I was working, had a family, was busy, and was this and that. So, decades went by, and although I've never been overweight, one day at a health check-up, I had a cholesterol reading of 12 (when it should be less than 5). So, I then started looking into what else to do to get it down besides medication. Losing weight was the most recommended option, but unless I wanted to amputate body parts, that wasn't an option for me. Exercise was recommended next, so I thought I'd do it then. I went on my first run, about 200 yards long, and my legs were aching for several weeks after that. But after months of thinking about it, my cholesterol wouldn't go down on its own... so now, five years later, it's just over 4, and I've done several marathons in under four hours.

This book is for people who want to achieve anything that will take them in the direction they want to go. Every great deed starts with a small step, and this non-fiction book gives you practical advice on achieving your goals and dreams. Whether it takes a month, six months, or six years, at least the direction is correct, and progress will be tangible, not *one day*, but very soon! I have experienced this very concretely myself:

- Graduating first as a rescue diver and then as an official diving instructor in just six months. At the same time, I got rid of my intense fear of deep water following Anthony Robbins' advice.

- A Ph.D. from business school (with top grades) in five years while working full-time. (Thanks to the Finnish Cultural Foundation for supporting my goal with a grant.)

- I overcame my fear of heights by parachuting from 15,000 feet in New Zealand, free climbing in America, and flying.

- I have designed and implemented customer feedback programs for six airlines and two major telecom operators in less than two years.

- After moving to England, I became a director in the world's largest integrated travel company in six years.

- At age 15, I started an international disc jockey career that lasted eight years and took me to play for up to 12,000 partygoers (in my first month, I played for an audience of 4,000).

- I have been coached and mentored by John C. Maxwell and Anthony Robbins have coached and mentored me for several years. Consequently, I have trained and coached over 20,000 people internationally in leadership and business.

- I ran a half marathon in under two hours, a marathon in under four hours, and an ultra-marathon within 1.5 years of starting the sport with no previous running experience.

- I have published six books with almost 50,000 readers and more than 200 blog posts with more than 200,000 readers in seven years. (Thanks to the Finnish Non-Fiction Writers for supporting this and my previous non-fiction books.)

- I have walked barefoot 30 feet on hot coals twice.

- I have published three software programs and numerous guided running routes for Garmin sports watches.

- I started, failed, and learned from five international start-ups that never amounted directly to anything.

- And most importantly, I found Jesus as my personal Savior and Redeemer, and I want to share Him with you, too.

And there's nothing on this list you can't do faster, better, and easier than me if you want to! The above list is not intended to put me on a pedestal, but you my dear reader: If an IT geek from Finland can do these things, how much more can you! This book is a compilation of the best lessons learned by me and others along the way that can save you both time and effort.

The book is divided into three parts. The first part focuses on building the foundations. It goes through the important things that contribute to and enable planned success.

The first part includes these foundational topics:

- **Sleep** well

- **Think** fast

- Move and eat your way to an energetic lifestyle

- Create the economic conditions you want

- **Ever** more advanced you

- **The reason** for keeping on going

- Recognize the facts

- Put things in order

In the book's first part, the order of the chapters does not matter, as these things will be helpful throughout the second part. You can return to these chapters again later, depending on the challenges you experience with your own goals. These chapters will also help you to think about and choose things to strive for (you may not know it yet, but you have enormous power to make things happen, and if you use it for the wrong things, you will not reach your optimal potential).

The book's second part focuses on a six-step process for achieving your chosen goals. In this part, the order of the chapters is essential, as one step leads to another.

The second part includes these process steps:

- Plan your way to success

- Start where you are

- Do enough of the right things

- Assess progress and development

- Go back towards the goal and enjoy the journey

- **Reset** and move on to new adventures

The third part of this book focuses on the timing of objectives. The timeframe chosen is six months because too short a timescale may not allow you to achieve anything significant, and too long a timeframe runs the risk of getting lost along the way and not getting there at all. Of course, you don't have to make your plan on a six-month timeline, but you can use a timeline that fits your plan and your life situation.

The book contains many exercises you can do alone or with friends.

Let's start with the book's first part, which focuses on building the foundations for success. Don't take the pressure of reading this book, but remember that your future is at stake ☺

Part 1. FROM ZERO

The chapters in this section are important foundations for getting to the process in the second part, just as they are for building a house. Without a strong enough foundation, you can burn yourself out trying to progress in an unsustainable manner. The advice in this part aims not to add to anyone's burden to achieve the best possible version of themselves but quite the opposite. The aim is to free you from all the vanity, noise, and time-wasting, and thus focus all your resources laser-sharply on what is truly important to you. The book also doesn't assume that you're starting from scratch (although the title might suggest that), but you'll certainly already have many important skills in your storage of life. Now, it's just a matter of taking an inventory and then restocking it before you start using it to pursue your dreams. However, there's a flaw in the previous metaphor: our stockpiles fill up on their own when we do the right things for the right reasons. Ask anyone happy with what they are doing. They hardly moan about expending energy doing such things. Of course, our energy stores are depleted quickly if we do things and are with people who consume or stress us. Just think of people who get married or divorced. Both processes take considerable time, energy, money, and effort. But one brings happiness to its participants, and the other unhappiness, even though the energy consumption is the same magnitude.

That's why the book's first part, ZERO, focuses on building your foundations. The foundations are built on eight important pillars that help you stay on track and work effectively:

- ◆ *Sleep efficiently:* many people underestimate the need for sleep for the human body. However, we are created so that sleep is a basic need for each of us. Our brains process information, and our bodies repair themselves when we sleep. You will recall that the Bible says that God created man in the image of Himself, and God rested on the seventh day. So, sleep is not laziness but necessary to increase efficiency.

- *Think quickly:* you may have heard the saying *do things more wisely rather than more.* Many things can be resolved quickly and easily by first considering how necessary it is to do them and then planning and evaluating the best solution for each situation.

- *Move and eat to energize yourself:* our bodies use a lot of energy, so we need to get it back correctly. In this chapter, we look at the impact of exercise and nutrition on our efficiency and how we can ensure we always have a full tank of working fuel.

- *Create the financial conditions you want: the* unfortunate fact about the world is that you can't do without money. So, in this chapter, we'll look at ways to build wealth without spending all your time on it (i.e., earning passive income). This is not a *get-rich-quick* scam, however, but a sustainable personal finance policy based on the wealth you have at your disposal.

- *An ever more evolved you: the* challenge and the salt of our lives is that we are never finished. There are always things where we can learn and become better. Even Olympic champions rarely win their sport multiple times because others have already advanced. This chapter will look at self-development, willpower, and self-discipline; these will help you achieve your goals.

- *Reason for perseverance:* all things worth striving for will be challenged. And you can only overcome difficulties if you have the motivation to keep going. Giving up is always the easier option available, but one we don't want to take. So, in this chapter, we'll look at your reasons for persevering and the practices that will help you on your chosen path.

- *Recognize the facts:* self-assessment is an essential part of development. In this chapter, we inventory your current physical, mental, and spiritual resources. We also consider what Donald Trump and Mother Teresa have in common.

- *Put things in order:* time is the world's greatest equalizer. The world's greatest time consumer is the greatest consumer of time. This chapter considers which things are worth your time and which you should say *no to*. This world is full of temptations to waste time, so we must remain vigilant not to waste our lives on vanities and unsatisfactory things and people.

I hope you haven't fallen asleep with this book yet so we can move on to the next chapter on the importance of sleep for our effectiveness.

Sleep well

This book chapter may sound contradictory; how can someone sleep their way to efficiency? But, humans are designed to get the right amount of sleep to stay fit. While the book aims to encourage and enable you to achieve significant goals relatively quickly, it does not mean increasing the time available, for example, by reducing sleep, as some motivational speakers encourage. Sleep is so important, however, that it is the first guiding chapter in this book.

Scientific research has shown that a minimal number (a fraction of 1%) of people have a gene[*] that allows them to stay active for long periods with 6 hours or less of sleep a night. So, the rest of us need to get the right amount of sleep (not too much and not too little) to optimize the energy that sleep brings, to improve memory, and to keep the brain functioning. Do you know how good a sleeper you are? You can find

---

[*] BHLHE41; https://www.ncbi.nlm.nih.gov/pmc/articles/PMC4096202

out by completing the sleep health test below. Put a cell in the box, one per line:

	Very rarely / never	Sometimes / occasionally	Usually / very often
Are you generally satisfied with your night's sleep?			
Do you stay refreshed enough to work all day?			
Are you often awake between 2 and 4 in the morning?			
Are you awake for less than half an hour between going to bed and waking up?			
Do you sleep 6-8 hours a night?			
	0 points	1 point	2 points

Give each question 0, 1, or 2 points depending on which column you chose for each question. You should score a minimum of 0 and a maximum of 10. Add up your score and write your result in the box below:

/ 10

According to a test described in a scientific journal, the closer you are to number 10 on a sleep health test, the better you get rest and energy from your sleep. Similarly, the closer you are to zero, the worse your sleep health score is. These test results matter because it's not just your success in achieving your goals that depend on them. In some situations, even your life may depend on sleep.

I have much experience with poor sleep and the problems it causes. I worked as an international disc jockey for eight years, and in the early days, I often drove from the venue to the hotel or back home after a gig. I usually had several nights of staying awake behind me, so it was easy to fall asleep at the wheel on my early morning journeys. I drove off the road three times and once got stuck in a deep ditch at -22 Fahrenheit when my Mercedes went into the woods after I fell asleep at the wheel. The situation was not helped by the fact that I had to do the gigs with half-dimmed lights because, at the same time, I was at the School of Embedded Systems Engineering at the Oulu University of Applied Sciences. Days were school, evenings I slept, and nights I played or drove. This was directly reflected in my school performance, as I did not get the best grades in my courses, although I did get full marks for the final thesis. My career as a disc jockey was already underway in secondary school. It was the same there, so I got relatively poor results in my exams there, too, and that's why I didn't get into the university I applied to, but ended up first at a university of applied sciences and only then, via the University of Turku, at the School of Business and Economics and then as a Ph.D. Had I slept and consequently my memory worked better, I could have saved a few years of my life, although, of course, all these experiences have been helpful to me. They have shaped my ability to pursue several professions at the highest level. Many people have asked me how I have been able to do all this, and my best advice is in this book. But I cannot recommend my former lifestyle to anyone, as it was not sustainable. Chronic sleep deprivation and the constant rush caused the first burnout when I was in my twenties and the second a few years later. I can no longer afford a third. If you haven't experienced burnout in your life so far, be thankful; it is of no use to anyone. That's why this book's advice focuses on achieving sustainable, effective results, and getting a good night's sleep is an important part of the process.

This book is written for young and old alike, and the advice and ideas work for all ages. This is also true for the sleep you get. It is a common belief that people need less sleep as they age, and many older people sleep very little. However, research shows that this is not the case and that we generally need around 7-8 hours of sleep a night. Older people need the same amount, but their ability to get this amount of sleep may be reduced by factors such as medication or health problems. People of all ages can have sleep problems, and these can be divided into three main areas:

- ◆ Reduced amount or quality of sleep

- ◆ Reduced sleep efficiency

- ◆ Interrupted timing of sleep stages

I won't go too deeply into the medical workings of sleep, as there are already several good books on it where you can read more about the biology, mechanics, and chemistry of sleep. But we need to know that our ability to sleep deteriorates as we age. So, we need to do things to help cope with the changes (as poor sleep directly impacts our physical and mental performance). In our twenties or so, we have good sleep habits (ask any parent how much they are annoyed by teenagers' long nights of sleep; perhaps out of jealousy?). The ability to get deep sleep is well maintained in normal adults until their forties, but it declines. The amount of deep sleep decreases, and the brain's sleep curves deteriorate. In our fifties, we get about 70% less deep sleep than when we were young if we do nothing about it! And Heaven help people in their seventies, who have lost up to 90% of their deep sleep. Thus, improving our sleep quality becomes more critical as we age. Unfortunately, it must also be said that some of these skills are not always in our hands from a medical point of view. A general deterioration of the brain (e.g., because of specific proteins) with age explains about 60% of sleep loss, and researchers are still looking for reasons for the remaining 40% (at least part of which is explained by increased levels of beta-amyloid, which is also known to contribute to Alzheimer's disease). According to the researchers' advice, brisk exercise, half an hour or more a day, is good for the brain and sleep of people of all ages and does not require a doctor's prescription.

How many days a week do you do at least half an hour of vigorous physical activity? Put your number in the box below:

I do brisk exercise _________ days a week.

Sleep has many effects on our lives, both physical and mental. A few decades after Christ's death and resurrection, the Roman writer Quintilian (35-100 AD) wrote in his notes about the effects of sleep on memory. He noted that a person who could not remember certain things the day before managed to remember them the next day after a good night's sleep. Modern science has proven this accurate, as sleep helps the brain store information acquired during the day. Sleep also has a positive effect on our bodies. The fastest man in the world, Usain Bolt, takes a nap before a race and did so a few hours before the race on the day he broke the world record for 300 feet. Sleep has been shown to improve the body's motor function and reduce stress injuries caused by sports. Statistics show that people who sleep an average of six hours a night have a 70% chance of sustaining a sports injury during a season, while those who sleep eight hours have only a 35% chance, half as much. Researchers looked at the recovery performance of more than 750 athletes after tough competitions and found that those who sleep less than six hours are around 30% more stressed the next day due to poorer recovery. Researchers have also found a link between weight gain and poor sleep. Some sources have gone quite a long way in saying that *you should sleep yourself thin*, although they are correct (if the calories you eat are within normal limits).

Many think they can sleep less during the week and catch up on sleep debt at weekends. Researchers tested the assumption and found that, unfortunately, there is no such thing as a sleep bank in the same way there is a time bank at work. They tested the performance of hundreds of people in situations where some slept a steady eight hours a night, and others slept less during the week and more on weekends. However, the researchers found that even three nights of normal sleep after a week of sleep deprivation was still not enough to restore their performance to normal levels. This means that the weekend is too short to reverse the damage caused by sleep deprivation. Sleeping eight hours a night is better than sleeping less during the week and more on weekends. If you're one of those who accumulate sleep debt during the week, you should switch out of this habit to increase your efficiency and improve your health (we'll discuss changing your habits later in this book).

So, how dangerous could such sleep debt be? Fortunately, we have scientists on this, too. They investigated the dangers of sleep debt by comparing the cognitive performance (i.e., brain function) of drunk people and people who don't sleep much. A well-rested person who drinks enough alcohol that they can no longer legally drive a car and a sober person who has woken up at 7 am, done a day's work, and gone out to party with friends for the night are at the same level of brain function at 4 am when they should be driving home. Indeed, car accidents are the leading cause of death in the West, and a sober, sleep-deprived guy is just as dangerous a driver as the person sitting next to him who has just drunk over the legal alcohol limit. In fact, after five hours of sleep, you are three times more likely to be involved in a crash, and after four hours, you are 11.5 times more likely. No wonder I hit the ditch many times after the DJ gigs before I realized I had to stop driving and staying up all night!

What about one broken heart?

Heart disease is a significant problem for Finns. According to the national health ministry, they still cause almost half of all deaths among working-age people in Finland, although mortality from cardiovascular diseases has fallen considerably since the 1970s. Together, they form the largest single group of causes of death. According to THL, the decline in coronary heart disease has been driven by improved lifestyles and the prevention and treatment of the diseases. The use of solvents and drugs, bypass surgery, and angioplasty have improved considerably in recent decades. And these are good ways to help when the situation is already advanced. But with enough sleep, we can reduce the likelihood of getting the condition in the first place. In 2011, researchers followed the sleep and health of more than half a million people of all ages worldwide. According to the statistics, the likelihood of getting heart problems or dying from heart problems increased by 45% among those who did not get enough sleep. In Japan, 4,000 people were followed for 14 years, and found that those who slept six hours or less were five times more likely to have a heart attack. And, of course, this likelihood only increases with age. People over 45 and sleeping less than six hours a night are twice as likely to have a heart attack compared to those who sleep the recommended 7-8 hours a night. This is linked to blood pressure, which does not settle sufficiently during short periods of sleep. I wonder how many people have high blood pressure directly linked to lack of sleep and physical activity? How is your blood pressure?

Your blood pressure:

Upper pressure _________ / _________ Lower pressure

mmHg

The recommended blood pressure is less than 129 mmHg for upper blood pressure and less than 84 mmHg for lower blood pressure.

In addition to heart problems, cancer is another common problem around the world. It's hard to believe the impact that sleep can have on avoiding this problem. That's why it's good that researchers have investigated this issue. According to Dr Michael Irwin (University of California), just one four-hour night's sleep reduces the number of cancer-fighting cells in the body. His study involved healthy young men, so it is not just a phenomenon in older people. His study showed a 70% drop in cancer-fighting cells in the body when men slept only from 3 am to 7 am. If there was more than one night of vigilance, the number of cells continued to fall. You can well imagine what happens to your body's immune system because of chronic sleep deprivation. We already know about this. Several studies have shown that people who regularly work shifts are more likely to develop cancer. Studies have shown an increase in breast and uterine cancers in women who work shifts and prostate cancers in men. The Danish government has even paid compensation to nurses and flight attendants, among others, on this basis. If you work shifts, you should pay special attention to ensure you get the recommended eight hours of sleep.

Losing weight (or, better even, achieving an optimal weight) is on the minds of many. Some argue that people could lose weight by staying awake longer because staying awake burns more calories than sleeping. Researchers have put this belief to the test and found that people consume almost the same number of calories while sleeping as while awake (the difference was, on average, about 150 kilocalories per day). So, staying awake does not help you lose weight, although it can significantly harm it. Studies show that those who sleep too little are likelier to indulge, eat unhealthily, and overeat. Cravings increase by 30-40% in those who sleep even an hour or two less than recommended. Sleep deprivation had less of an effect on protein-rich foods (such as beans, fish, and meat), with cravings increasing by only 10-15% over the same period of sleep deprivation. So, for healthy weight management, it is essential to get the right amount of sleep consistently each night (and to eat no more calories than you consume).

Can a person sleep too much, then? Some studies have claimed that sleeping too long is bad for you, too. However, these studies have been challenged because of the assumptions they use. For example, the studies used people with serious health problems such as pneumonia or cancer. The body encourages people to sleep more in such situations to give them time to heal. This, in turn, increases the average amount of sleep these people get. Of course, sleep does not cure all diseases. When the Lord wants to call us out of this world, it will happen independently of us. However, sleep studies have shown that healthy people do not gain significantly more health benefits from sleeping more. So, it would be best to aim for a steady night's sleep of around eight hours to wake up refreshed and tackle the day's tasks without feeling too tired.

Many have read about the effects of blue light and screens on sleep. The generally accepted recommendation is to avoid blue light sources such as TV, computers, mobile phones, and tablets at least a few hours before bedtime. These devices directly affect melatonin production, which in turn facilitates sleep. Studies show that around 90% of people use some form of blue light source up to an hour before bedtime (e.g., browsing the web on their mobile phone in bed). This has an approximately 23% reducing effect on melatonin production. Another study measured the melatonin levels of several hundred people at night. Half of the group read a paper book before bed, and the other half used a tablet to read the same book. The group that used the electronic device had half the melatonin levels three hours after bedtime than those who read a paper book. Thus, those who had used the tablet did not get deep sleep until mid-morning, while those who had read the paper book were already asleep by midnight. Those who used an electronic device also took longer to fall asleep. It is much more helpful to read magazines or paper books in the evening and not use electronic devices in the last three hours before bed. I know that's quite a challenge for all of us!

What about the effect of alcohol on sleep? Isn't having a little nightcap to get some sleep an age-old habit? This belief is complete nonsense and the result of misunderstood properties of alcohol. Alcohol indeed counts as a sedative. It prevents neurons in the brain from sending the electrical impulses they would send without alcohol. This is a little puzzling because often when we drink alcohol, it seems more like a stimulant and a social stimulant than a sedative. This is explained by the fact that alcohol initially affects the brain, mainly in the prefrontal cortex. This area of the brain regulates our impulses and behavior. Thus, in the early stages of alcohol exposure, this sub-region is the first to change, causing relaxation and increasing feelings of social interaction (for example, just one glass of alcohol lowers a person's sexual inhibitions). But as time passes and the effect of alcohol spreads to other parts of the brain, it starts to affect their functioning, too. This is why drunk people easily stumble, talk weirdly, and do everything else with half-darkened light bulbs. And so, going to bed drunk is not the equivalent of a typical night's sleep but is closer to the kind of anesthesia used in hospitals. Because the effect of alcohol on the brain varies over time, people wake up several times during the night and do not enter a deep sleep state. It's easy to miss these awakenings when drunk, but it's rare to wake up in the morning after a night of drinking to feel refreshed. Students are good guinea pigs in this area, and one study found that students who drank forgot about 40% more of what they had learned at school the previous day than their sober peers. This is due to the critical role of sleep in memory, discussed earlier. Interrupted, light sleep does not help the brain store information. So, if you've been taking nightcaps to improve your sleep, I recommend that in the future, you cut out alcohol and get a good night's sleep. You should also avoid drinking alcohol for several days before an exam or when you are studying.

Sleep conditions have an impact on the amount and quality of sleep. In Finland, homes are generally quite warm (72-74 Fahrenheit) compared to, for example, England (64-68F). In Finland, people also wear pajamas and sleep under a thick blanket. In such conditions, researchers recommend a bedroom of around 66F. This may come as a bit of a surprise, as it feels pretty cool at first. We found the first few weeks quite cold when we arrived in England, as 66F is the average temperature. But after getting used to this and visiting Finland, we found that the interiors in most houses were too warm. Of course, bedrooms and interiors should not be allowed to get too cold (below 64F), making them more prone to respiratory infections and mold. However, a bedroom temperature of around 66F has generally been found to be suitable for optimizing sleep.

We have already covered sleep from the perspective of many substances, so let's go over the potential benefits and known harms of sleeping pills. Compared to Americans, Finnish use of sleeping pills is moderate. But the effects are the same for those who go down this road regardless of nationality. First, the desired effect of sleeping pills is, at best, fragile and generally counterproductive. They have the same effect as alcohol, i.e., from a brain-curve perspective, they put the brain in a state more akin to hospital anesthesia than an actual sleep state. Thus, they do not provide a genuine, restorative rest but rather bang a club on the head to temporarily remove consciousness. Proper sleep is an active state in the brain, where REM and NREM sleep alternate; the brain stores memories and processes information. Many people mistakenly believe that we do nothing when we sleep. However, under the influence of sleeping pills and alcohol, some brain activity is blocked, making it more like an inactive state than a natural sleep. Not only is there currently no medicine that can induce a state in the brain like genuine sleep, but many sleeping pills cause stupor that can persist the next day. This leads to a search for stimulants such as coffee, which in turn makes it more difficult to sleep the following night. Sleeping pills also cause chronic insomnia for many people, i.e., they can no longer sleep without sleeping pills. Their sleep without medication can be even worse than before they started taking the drugs (again due to the addictive properties of the drugs). One study compared 65 of the most common sleeping pills with placebo drugs (i.e., the same but without active ingredients) in a total of 4,500 people. Although people reported falling asleep about 10-30 minutes faster on average with the drugs, the brain curves showed the same outcome between those taking the drugs and those taking the placebo. Thus, the study found that sleeping pills provide very mild benefits compared to the significant harms they cause (addiction, stupor, and higher mortality). What is interesting about the statistics is that people who take sleeping pills are, on average, 4.5 times more likely to die over 2.5 years. This mortality rate was also proportional to the amount of sleeping pills taken. People who consumed an average of 150 pills per year were 5.3 times more likely to die over this time. Even those who took a maximum of 20 pills per year had a mortality rate 3.5 times higher than those who did not take sleeping pills at all.

So, how can we improve the quantity and quality of our sleep? Here's a refresher on the ways to improve your sleep:

- **Do not drink coffee or tea** from the afternoon onwards (however, herbal teas without caffeine, such as Chamomile or Rooibos, may be suitable before bedtime).

- **Lower the temperature** in your bedroom to around 66 Fahrenheit.

- **Do not use LED lights, tablets, TVs, mobile phones,** or other electronic sources that emit blue light for a few hours before bedtime.

- **Do not use sleeping pills, alcohol, tobacco**, snuff, or drugs to improve your sleep quality.

- **Meditate and calm your mind naturally** before going to bed. Calm down towards evening and reduce the rush so you can go to bed rested.

- **Avoid strenuous exercise** for a few hours before bedtime. However, remember to do at least half an hour of brisk daily exercise.

- **Take a warm bath** or shower 1-2 hours before bedtime.

- **Aim for around eight hours of sleep** a night (or whatever suits you).

- **Keep a regular sleep schedule** (go to bed and wake up at the same time as much as possible).

- **Avoid taking a nap** (especially after 3 pm) if it makes it difficult to go to bed at night, but take a nap if it helps you.

- **Keep clocks out of sight** in the bedroom so you don't have to look at the clock at night if you happen to wake up.

- **Use blackout curtains** in your bedroom.

- **Do not spend time in** bed other than when you are asleep (i.e., do not read in bed).

- **Avoid heavy meals and excessive drinking** before bedtime.

- If you take medicines regularly, check how they affect your sleep and time them so they don't prevent you from sleeping well (for example, medication for asthma, heart disease, and high blood pressure can affect your sleep).

- Don't toss and turn in bed trying to force yourself to sleep. If you don't fall asleep in half an hour, get up, do something relaxing, and go back to bed when you feel tired again. The next day, think about improving your routine to optimize your sleep.

With these tips, I wish you an excellent night's sleep next night. Next, we will continue improving our brains' efficiency when we are awake.

Think fast

Anthony *"Tony"* Robbins is one of the world's most successful motivational speakers, adding value to millions worldwide. I have also taken his courses and read and listened to almost all his material. Tony even persuaded one of his friends to mentor me for a year. One of the biggest things I learned from this great opportunity was that we can achieve anything, and not everything we want is worth achieving. You've probably heard the saying *be careful what you wish for because it might come true*, and it's true. Therefore, knowing yourself and what makes you happy is worth discovering. Often, the things we think will bring us happiness (like winning the lottery, riches, loves, nice cars, big muscles, beautiful looks, and so on) turn out to be empty compared to what we need (like security and sustenance, the importance of our own lives, connection with our Creator and other people, development, and positive contribution to the lives of others). Indeed, many people are lost because they pursue things that do not bring absolute, lasting satisfaction. Many don't know what else to do or are blinded by the world's desires. So, to achieve real success in this world, the following four main steps are needed:

- **Define very precisely what you want to achieve**. Thoroughly understand the desire, its need, and why it is so important to you. Make sure that your passion is aligned with your life values.

- **Get from the heart of the matter to action.** Without action, you won't get the desired results (but remember that inaction has consequences too).

- **Measure the impact of your progress and actions on your goal.** Continually assess where you are on the path and where it takes you.

- **Continue and change your action plan and activities until you reach your goal.**

I understand if this doesn't sound sexy to you. Of course, a magic button would be a much more pleasant alternative. But until it is found, we all must do whatever it takes to get where we want to be. And that usually means different amounts and ways of working for each of us because we are all different and come from different starting points. The better you define your mindset, beliefs, actions, metrics, and accountability, the more likely you are to get there despite circumstances and adversity.

What we believe about things, people, ourselves, and the world is essential because beliefs guide our daily actions and decisions. Therefore, the correct beliefs lead us more confidently to our destination. It is recommended to program your brain with beliefs such as these:

- I take responsibility for everything that happens and everything I do.

- I am responsible to myself, other people, and my Creator.

- Everything happens for a reason: to further my goals.

- Everything is a learning experience; there are no failures.

- I don't need to understand and know everything to make a difference.

- People want to help me.

- It's fun, and it gives me strength.

- Success comes from commitment.

- I always do my best and a little bit on top.

The biggest favor you can do yourself is to instill these beliefs and use them automatically in all situations. This book will explore how to develop your mindsets and habits to achieve your goals (more on those in future chapters). Stephen R. Covey has written an excellent book, *The Road to Success - 7 Practices for Personal Growth*, which is well worth reading (or listening to as an audiobook). Stephen advises focusing more on developing our habits and processes rather than chasing one-off successes or changes. This principle is extremely important for personal development and realization, as it can help you succeed in any situation. The seven ways Stephen recommends are:

- **Be proactive - take the initiative.** Some play on the pitch and many sit in the stands, but all the goals are scored on the pitch.

- **Define your goals and focus on them.** It's better to do a few things well than dozens of things mediocre.

- **Prioritize and spend your time on the most important ones.** Anything else is likely to be a waste of time.

- **Take others into account and build your success *on the win-win* principle.** Don't build your success on the suffering of others.

- **Understand first and then be understood.** We have two ears and one mouth for a reason, so we use them in that proportion.

- **Do things in cooperation with others.** It's fun, and it's challenging enough to go it alone.

- **Constantly improve yourself.** As the world moves forward, so must you.

- **Add value for others.** Our economic and social well-being is proportional to the value we add to others.

You may have noticed that the list above contains eight items instead of seven. The last one is from Stephen's recent book, where he added one more habit. These eight principles enable you to achieve the results you desire. Success will rarely come knocking on anyone's door without us taking the initiative (we'll go through the probability of winning the lottery later, but even the unlikelihood of winning the lottery requires you to buy a lottery ticket first, which I don't recommend). We need to change our beliefs about ourselves and the world around us to support moving forward and focusing on the right things in any circumstance:

- Instead of saying you can't or don't know what to do, ask what options you must make happen.

- Instead of just being content with yourself as you are now, know that you can continually improve yourself and your habits and change your thinking.

- Instead of letting others determine what you do and how you feel, decide how you let things affect you. While we can't always influence what happens, we can always influence how we think about it.

- Instead of thinking you must do something, decide that you want to do those things.

Setting goals and focusing your energy on them is a central theme. Your life is too short to pursue meaningless, small, and unsatisfying things. Many of our desires reflect what we see on TV and in the pages of magazines, but that doesn't mean they are our true, deep desires. We need to become aware of who we are and what we want and then remove the other noise around us. You don't need diamond earrings and a revealing outfit to eat Magnum ice cream like Eva Longoria! And eating Magnum ice cream doesn't give you any more of the essence of Eva (which was the connotation this ad was trying to create at the time[*]). Instead, think about what is important to you and what you want to spend a little time on this earth doing. According to the Bible, every person has their place and purpose, so it pays to find your place and focus on your mission.

And because our time is limited, making the best use of it is our duty to ourselves and our loved ones. Don't waste your time on things that don't move you towards your goals and don't add value to others. The curse of today is the constant interruptions from emails, text messages, social media, and other communication tools. Our thoughts and actions are constantly interrupted by various stimuli. Another complication in this world is the misunderstood #*efficiencyeconomy*. People are deluded into thinking that the more they do, the more they get done. But we realize it is often the other way around, so we protect our time.

There are very few things in this world that you can do in complete isolation. So, communication skills are more critical than ever because we are in constant contact with other people. Assumptions are dangerous, so never assume anything. There are so many of us humans, and everyone thinks differently, even those with the same mind. So, always seek first to understand and only then to be understood. Listen to what others say and think about what they mean. And if you don't know, ask. One good example from Finland is the new traffic control radar launched in 2019. When these came out, people were told by the media that we should watch out for these new radars because they can

---

lead to a speeding ticket already 450 feet away from the camera. However, they do not. The picture used to justify the fine is only taken at about 90 feet from the car, and only the speed at which the photo was taken is recorded. The widespread misunderstanding about these new speed cameras is that the new radars could measure the speed of a vehicle up to 450 feet away, but a photograph taken at this distance would be so blurred that no one could be fined based on it. So, the old method of braking at the last moment still works, although it is worth bearing in mind that the distance to be covered is twice as long as the old 45 feet and that the new radar can photograph several cars and lanes simultaneously.

In the early days of the Coronavirus in 2020, there were widespread rumors of a conspiracy theory that the Coronavirus had been developed to test 5G communications networks. People then went about destroying 5G masts in a frenzy. Although the morale of this world seems to be getting weaker yearly, these are just a few examples of the power of misunderstanding.

What kind of lumberjack are you?

Self-development is one of the best gifts you can give yourself and others. Don't be a lumberjack who spends one's days sawing wood slower and slower. Why? Because he doesn't have time to stop and sharpen the saw blade, the work slows down moment by moment as the saw gets dull. You've probably seen former sportsmen and women who were basking in the glow of gold medals a decade ago and nowadays drown their days in the bottom of a beer mug in a local pub. In the world of management consulting, they say you're only as good as your last project. This applies to our lives, too. It doesn't matter how fit you were in the army if you haven't moved much in the last few decades. So, continuously take care of yourself mentally, physically, and spiritually.

Perhaps the title of this chapter, *Think Fast,* is a little misleading, as the first word implies that you should do all the thinking. The maximum human life span is about 120 years[*] (and for most people, much less), part of which is spent in childhood and part in old age. Time is not always enough to learn all the facts and details the hard way to achieve significant results. In Finland, for example, it is easy to take a good education for granted when hundreds of millions of children worldwide do not even have access to primary school. Learning from others and applying knowledge to one's needs is vital in developing rapid realization. For me, schooling went a little too far, as after high school, I graduated as an embedded information systems engineer, a Bachelor of Science, a Master of Philosophy, and even a doctorate and an MBA. On top of that, I studied almost a full degree in Chinese language and culture. In England, for example, most people have gone to school up to a Bachelor's level. In contrast, in Finland, most people who have a university education go on to a Master's degree. And as we said earlier, education is no guarantee of success. But it can speed up or slow down your progress towards your goals, depending on how well it fits in with what you are aiming for. Of course, schooling is not the only way to learn things or even the best way in some situations. In today's world, all existing knowledge is literally at your fingertips. Online training, YouTube videos, books, magazines, interviews, and studies all support learning. Even for this book, more than 10,000 pages of non-fiction, hundreds of hours of educational videos, and hundreds of hours of discussions with experts have been done. For a successful person, learning is not a one-off exercise that ends with a certificate in hand but a life-long attitude, a curiosity that needs to be constantly quenched with new knowledge.

If your goals require thinking skills, it is worth taking care of your ability to think quickly. Several things can help you do this, and by combining them, you can ensure that your brain stays in a stress-free and efficient state. Here's a list of things you can do to maintain an effective mindset:

- ♦ Move briskly. We will discuss the implications of this in more detail in the next chapter.

---

[*] https://en.wikipedia.org/wiki/List_of_the_verified_oldest_people

- Eat omega-3 acids, either in the form of pills or preferably in the form of nuts or seeds. It helps the brain to work chemically in the right way.

- Limit how much you do at a time. More hours do not mean more efficiency; the opposite is true. Studies show that taking breaks often enough helps increase efficiency by 10% or more. According to scientific studies, you should take a 17-minute break after every 52 minutes of work. You can use your phone's timer (or mobile apps to track breaks) to take a break.

- Laugh as often as possible. Watch funny cat videos at. Laughing quickly reduces the stress hormone and increases endorphins, which keep the brain chemically active. Research shows that after about half an hour of watching funny videos, the brain's stress hormone drops by about 67%, and adrenaline drops by about 35%.

- I know this is tough advice for many, but avoid alcohol, snuff, tobacco, drugs, energy drinks, and coffee. They all negatively affect the chemical functioning of the brain.

- Set yourself clear, motivating goals. Just knowing and wanting these goals will make you more effective.

- If something goes wrong or doesn't work, don't blame yourself or the circumstances, but technically, analyze what exactly went wrong and how you will fix it in the future. This will help you focus on solving the problem rather than dwelling on it, thus reducing the stress caused by problems.

- Don't criticize or berate yourself (or others). This is sometimes difficult for us, but self-deprecation impairs thinking and increases stress hormones and is therefore unsuitable for our purposes. Focus more on what you need to do next than on what you could have done. Also, don't waste your energy blaming others or worrying about the past.

- Schedule your promises, decisions, and intentions as precisely as possible. Research shows vague or distant goals are less likely to be met than those with a specific date or time. For example, people who want to retire in 30 years start saving money four times later than those who plan to retire in 10,950 days (the exact timeframe but more specific). This creates a sense of urgency in the mind, so you are likelier to stick to your guns. For example, I ran a half marathon in under two hours, and the very next day, I set a goal to run a marathon in 120 days in under four hours. Even though my legs were still sore, I did my first light training run the next day as planned.

- Get the right amount of sleep. The right amount is personal, although different studies give figures between seven and eight hours. You, too, can find your number by using a sleep meter and a diary so you can optimize your sleep to suit you. Daytime naps are also good if they are neither too long nor too late. Generally, a power nap of about 20 minutes is recommended, depending on your needs. However, as we have said many times, don't use coffee or energy drinks to feel refreshed, but focus on optimizing your sleep rhythm.

- When you come up with ideas, don't try to get good ideas - any idea will do. The more ideas you come up with, the more likely there will be good ones. Research shows that the number of good ideas is directly proportional to the number of ideas. Getting straight to the good ideas is tricky, so you'll see them more quickly if you don't limit your thinking.

- One very effective way to start a task again is to stop in the middle of a task and not finish it if it is impossible to complete it entirely. This psychological phenomenon is called Zeigarnik (he was a researcher in the 1920s at the University of Berlin). People's brains send out reminders at regular intervals (some call this nagging their brains) about unfinished tasks. These reminders stop when you finish. For example, when I write a book, I never stop writing when a chapter or section is finished, but I stop in the middle of a sentence or chapter. That way, when I return to writing, I can pick up where I left off rather than start over with something new. It makes it faster to get up to speed. This same principle works effectively with other things. Listening to a well-known song is an exciting and easy way to test this phenomenon. Stop the song at the appropriate chorus, and your brain will almost certainly continue to play the song in your head after that. But then listen to the whole song until the end, and your brain will stop because this task was completed. Sometimes, you can try this trick when you can't get a song out of your head.

♦ Doing many things simultaneously doesn't work, so don't try. I chant the mantra *'do one thing at a time, many in a row'* several times a day to keep my focus on the thing I need to do at that moment. There is an exception to this, however, when multi-tasking is helpful. If you need to think about something, you'll be more effective if you're doing something physical that requires very little thinking. For example, Agatha Christie used to think about plot outlines for her books while she washed her clothes. Tamami Nakano, a researcher at Osaka University, has studied this issue and found that it is related to the brain's ability to switch between the active and passive network that gives the brain time to imagine things while the body is doing something. Just make sure the physical activity isn't demanding on the brain, and you can come up with your best ideas while doing the laundry!

♦ Morning is the most productive time of the day, so spend it on the things that matter most. Don't answer emails or do anything else in the morning; use the time to get on with the things that matter most. Energy levels drop towards the evening so you can do the less important things with half-dimmed lights.

- Write things in story form rather than in lists or a few words. Stories make your brain more active and imaginative, which helps you solve problems.

Thinking fast is about looking for solutions outside the box. Consider, for example, what Netflix once did for Blockbusters. Traditional video rental companies had fixed costs for DVD storage, staff, and premises. Netflix made the service easier and faster for customers (no more rushing to Blockbusters in the pouring rain). Similarly, Usain Bolt added naps to his training and racing routine to boost his running performance. These are examples of thinking and realizing outside the box. How could you inspire your brain to think more effectively about issues, challenges, and goals? Try these psychological tools to get your brain looking for new ideas:

- Look at it from different angles: how it looks to me, to the recipient, to onlookers, to the uninformed, to the authorities, to competitors, and so on.

- Ask other people how they would solve the same problem.

- Create artificial constraints and then solve them. Limit how much time, money, or other things you have at your disposal. This may seem odd, but it helps to look at it from a different perspective.

- Compare what you and others doing this (or similar) are using (the idea is not necessarily to copy from them, but also to find gaps).

- Turn it into a question and find the answer. For example, I want to lose 40 pounds, which can be turned into a question: How can I lose 40 pounds of weight?

- Don't judge or criticize any ideas. As stated, the more options you have, the more likely you are to find the best one.

- Focus on the positive and forward-looking aspects, saying *yes and we could,* rather than the limiting, negative thinking of *no, because,* or *but.*

We will continue this discussion on creative problem-solving later in this book. The goal of thinking fast is to find new ways of thinking about the same things so that you can find the best ways to achieve your goals. Next, we'll look at the role of exercise and nutrition in coping.

Move and eat your way to an energetic lifestyle.

What would be your first recommendation if you were asked how to get a healthier, better-functioning brain? Many would mention Sudoku, crosswords, and other brain teasers. And, of course, challenging your brain like that helps keep it active, no problem. But few would give the most practical advice: to increase exercise and focus on proper nutrition. Thirty minutes of effective exercise three or more times a week can reduce the chance of developing Alzheimer's disease by more than 20%. Even 10 minutes of effective exercise stimulates the brain more than a cup of coffee or a can of energy drink (which is why I went for a quick run around the local park before I started writing this chapter).

We all know that feeling after a hard day at work or school when you feel like you can't think about anything anymore. This is due to the high levels of cortisol, the stress hormone, that has built up in the brain. Stress hormones help during the day by keeping blood pressure and blood sugar levels high to energize the brain and stay alert. This is why typically relaxing activities such as reading, crafts, and socializing don't always help lower stress levels because of a chemical imbalance in the brain. This balance can be restored by reducing the amount of stress hormones in the brain and is most effectively achieved through brisk exercise. However, the benefits of exercise are not limited to hormone control alone; it also increases the amount of grey matter in the brain. Women and men have equal amounts of grey matter, and in the cortex of a healthy person, there is a balance between programmed cell death and regeneration and stimuli from external conditions and learning. The grey matter layer of the brain thins between the ages of 8 and 23, but the amount of brain matter remains the same because the density of grey matter increases as the layer thins. However, after age 30, the amount of grey matter starts to decrease again naturally. So, you could say that vigorous exercise is like turning back time in the brain because it promotes the growth of grey matter. Have you noticed similarities between who you call an iron granny or a steelhead and how active they are? This activity increases physical fitness and, according to science, helps avoid memory problems and stay mentally alert.

Finland maintains an internationally unique database of identical twins. They have a register of more than 10,000 identical twins, so it was not difficult for researchers to find pairs where one twin is active in sports and the other is not. When they looked at these twins' physical and mental abilities, it became pretty clear that the active twins had more grey matter, greater flexibility in their thinking, and appeared physically healthier. Thus, Dr Urho Kujala of the University of Jyväskylä concluded that vigorous exercise also positively affects people's thinking abilities and not just their physics. So, if you are not motivated to exercise by physical development, the next time you go for a run, remind yourself that you are also exercising your brain!

Sermon for the sickbed

Human health is a complex issue with many opinions. However, cumbersome diets and programs fail in the long run and bring limited benefits because they are too difficult to follow. So, finding the right balance is essential to living a holistic, healthy life, considering exercise, nutrition, and mental well-being. Bacteria and viruses, both beneficial and harmful, are everywhere, so it is often up to your own body and resistance whether you get an actual disease. Many factors influence how sick we get, such as:

- Stress.

- The strength and number of negative emotions (such as sadness, anger, resentment, etc.).

- Maintaining physical, mental, and spiritual balance.

- My views on health.

- Pollution and other environmental factors.

- Food quality and quantity.

- Quality and quantity of physical activity.

- Positive thinking and attitude towards life.

The quality of physical activity significantly impacts the benefits it brings. According to an article published in New Scientist (4/2020), the very act of walking or running has a direct effect on lifespan. According to researchers at the University of Iowa, people who run for two hours a week between the ages of 44 and 80 spend about half a year running. According to statistics, this adds about three years to their life expectancy on top of half a year of running. In simpler terms, every hour you run adds about seven more hours to your life. Walking doesn't have the same effect.

What's also interesting is that you don't have to overdo it. Of course, if you run more than two hours a week, you'll get a bit more benefit, but the more you run, the smaller this benefit becomes. It's not necessary to run 10 hours a week to get an extra 70 hours because that's not how it seems to work, according to researchers. Likewise, don't be discouraged if you can't run for two hours a week because any time you run for two hours will provide an additional benefit compared to not running at all. Just 15 minutes of daily vigorous exercise reduces the risk of death by 10% compared to people in the same age group who do not exercise vigorously.

In addition to running, you can do practical muscle exercises indoors (especially in bad weather, which some people find an excellent excuse not to exercise). Perhaps you've heard of the so-called seven-minute workout? The 12-minute workout below is a modified version of the original, with a back muscle workout and a change in timing to make this workout quick and easy to do in a specific order. I do this workout first thing in the morning and on my lunch break if possible. The program consists of the following movements for 50 seconds with a 15-second break between each movement:

1. *Fork jumps:* stand up straight with your legs in a hip-width apart position. Jump as high as possible while opening your legs and raising your arms. Lower into a wide-branch position and clap your hands together over your head. Immediately jump back to the starting position and repeat. Keep the tempo brisk.

2. *Sitting against the wall:* sit with your back against the wall as if sitting on a chair, legs at a 90-degree angle.

3. *Push-ups:* do as many as you can in 50 seconds.

4. *Abdominal muscle movements:* do as many as you can in 50 seconds.

5. *Stand up on a chair and return to the floor: alternate the starting leg and do as many ascents and descents as possible.*

6. *Squats:* sit down as if you were sitting on a chair with your feet at a 90-degree angle and stand back up. Do as many squats as you can at that time. Make sure your knees don't go in front of your toes.

7. *Extensions:* stand in front and back to the bench. Place your hands on the outside edge of the bench. Lower as low as you can and rise using the strength of your extensors (not your legs). Do as many as you can.

8. *Back muscles:* lie on the floor on your stomach. Lie on your back on your back and lift your arms and legs in the air at the same time; feel the muscles contract in your back, and lower your arms and legs back to the floor. Repeat as many times as you can.

9. *Plank:* Get into a plank position with only your elbows, forearms, palms, and toes touching the ground. Stay in this position for 50 seconds.

10. *Side plank left:* Go to the floor on your left side and stand up on your left arm and left leg. Stay in position for 50 seconds.

11. *Rib right:* Repeat on the right side.

The moves above are not complicated, but if you don't know the correct technique to perform each move, I recommend you look online for instructions and ensure you are doing the moves with the correct method. Doing them incorrectly can cause problems with muscles or joints.

The instructions in this book are not just for the young and physically able. It is true that with age, the body can start to break down, and there is nothing you can do about it (and there is no point in hindsight here). However, few people have their bodies so broken down that they can't do anything about it. However, for some older people, the challenge of mobility is more mental than physical. Many seniors worldwide are breaking their own limits and world records. For example, in February 2020, George Hood, a former Marine, broke the world record for the plank in 8 hours, 15 minutes, and 15 seconds. He was 62 years old when he did this. Of course, it's fair to say that he already had a lifelong strong fitness background based on his professional military career, so the result may not be directly comparable to yours or mine. But whatever his background, setting such a record at over 60 tells us all that it is possible to do it as an older person and not just as a young musclehead. And what do you think George will do next? *Move into a rocking chair to spend his retirement years?* Of course not; he wants to break the world record for the number of push-ups in one hour. The current record is 2 806 push-ups per hour. And it doesn't matter whether George succeeds or fails; such a goal will keep him motivated to keep fit and mentally sharp. George's mindset is precisely why I wanted to write this book. We can beat ourselves (and sometimes others along the way)!

Another good example is Englishwoman Edwina *"Eddie"* Blocklesby, a 76-year-old grandmother of four. Eddie has no background as a professional fighter; in fact, she only started exercising at the age of 53. And fitness took Eddie by storm. At 62, she ran a marathon at 3:45 that anyone would be proud of. Since then, she has won several challenging Ironman races in her age group (he is by no means the only one in the world who is exercising at a ripe old age!). Eddie says that fitness has taught her that getting older doesn't mean she (or we) must slow down. Eddie says every race she participates in gives her so much energy that it keeps her motivated for the next one. In the summer of 2020, Eddie was going to challenge an American grandmother, 75-year-old Dexter Yeats, in Australia in a race that involved swimming 2.5 miles, cycling 121 miles, and running 26 miles. Unfortunately, the coronavirus postponed these plans, but if nothing else, this proves that age is just a number! And if the exploits of these "youngsters" sound incredible, in 2012, an 82-year-old Catholic nun won the race! Eddie has more muscle than many twenty-somethings. Eddie's engaging personality and energy are in a class of their own. We can only pray that you and I could be as fit and inspiring at that age. In her fifties, Eddie's knee started tearing up and causing problems in every race (which is why she switched from just running to triathlons, which include swimming and cycling to avoid putting too much strain on the knee). Perhaps someone else would have given up the sport altogether at that point? Here are Eddie's top tips for success:

- *Make exercise a social event.* Find like-minded friends to hang out and hang out with. Then, challenge each other, step by step, to do better. In Eddie's own words, one of the big motivators for her to go out and exercise with others is the pub waiting at the end of the run to socialize.

- *Get out more.* As well as fresh air, you can enjoy nature and scenery. Choose your route so you get aesthetic pleasure as well as exercise. Stroll in the woods, cycle on dirt roads, exercise on the beach, and run in the parks.

- *Make fitness fun!* This is very important; no one can stand up with disgusting exercise. So, find ways to make it fun, and remember that laughter prolongs life.

Follow Eddie's lead, put on our running shoes, give a shout-out to a friend, and head out for some fun exercise. And m*eet us in the park, not on the bench but on the trail!*

Today's smartwatches (such as Garmin, Suunto, and Polar) make it easy to measure your fitness level. It's worth getting a watch that measures your steps and activity. Good smartwatches can also guide you with fitness programs that adapt to your performance. That way, you can quickly get started and won't be overwhelmed immediately. While this book is intended primarily as a strategy guide to help you beat yourself up and meet the challenging goals you want, it also includes practical programs you can follow if they work for you on the page. That's why, at the end of this book, an eight-week fitness program that is very effective, based on the advice of America's elite soldiers, is included. If you want to challenge yourself to exercise, try this program or make your own version.

If I had known the positive impact of exercise on my mental well-being, I would probably (or so I tell myself) have started active exercise much earlier. A friend of mine once said that *some people have chosen to develop their bodies and some of their brains.* I kept that as my mantra for too long, especially when doing my PhD thesis. It sounded like the perfect excuse. But I only learned later that the two things come together. For me, exercise has also contributed to brain function and mental well-being, as we said in the previous chapter. When you exercise, you can't dwell on things in your mind; the focus goes on the physique. And that is relaxing (and healthier than alcohol, for example). My sport was also supported by a British life insurance company offering free Starbucks drinks and Cineworld movie tickets for exercise. They tracked activities through a Garmin watch. In practice, this reward made me a runner, too, and I hope that Finnish insurance companies will start to catch on more quickly. Perhaps you can make this your version, where you don't allow yourself a delicious cup of cocoa until you've done at least half an hour of brisk exercise (you can also earn a 'perk' for tomorrow).

What kind of goals should you set for yourself? It depends entirely on the type of exercise you like and the level of fitness you want for yourself. The recommendation is a minimum of half an hour of brisk daily exercise. This will give you the health benefits you need without excessive toil. However, remember that brisk exercise means a level of movement that will leave you panting and perhaps even sweating. Unfortunately, a leisurely walk in the park won't give you enough physical health benefits, although it's good for the mind. My own fitness goals are currently as follows (they will have changed by the time you read this):

- ♦ Swimming: 1,300 feet in less than 9 minutes using the combat style of swimming.

- ♦ Swimming: 2 miles in less than 80 minutes.

- ♦ Free diving over 150 feet (maximum depth of 15 feet).

- ♦ Basic fitness: 100 push-ups.

- ♦ Basic fitness: abdominal muscles 100.

- ♦ Basic fitness: chin-ups 25.

- ♦ Basic fitness: plank for more than 5 minutes.

- ♦ Basic fitness: hanging from the tango for more than 2 minutes.

- ♦ Running: 3 miles in under 30 minutes.

- ♦ Running: 6 miles in under 60 minutes.

- ♦ Running: half marathon under 2 hours and marathon under 4 hours.

- ♦ Mobility: stretching every day.

The above targets are, therefore, not one-off, but overall fitness targets. Once I have completed all these individually, I will train to maintain fitness to complete any of these at any time. In addition to this, I also run ultramarathons, but I didn't include goals related to those. You may have also noticed hanging from a pole as one of the goals. Some beaches, for example, in Bulgaria, have a challenge: if you can hang from a pole for two minutes, you get 50 dollars, and if you can't, you pay for it. So, I added this goal as a small earning opportunity on a holiday trip (and it also helps with chin-ups). What about you?

What fitness goals do you have or want to set for yourself?
Write them in this box:

In addition to exercise, there are other ways to promote your health:

- **Eat regularly.** Excessive fasting or overeating takes energy away from thinking about food. It's better to eat at regular intervals, with appropriate portion sizes. Eat healthy, plant-rich, real food. Keep meat to a minimum, and get your protein from beans and dark green vegetables.

- **Eat lightly.** Back in the day, when I tried vegan and vegetarian diets, the biggest benefit I found was getting rid of my afternoon sweet tooth. If you eat a big lunch or a lot of meat, the blood goes to your digestive system. But healthy food gives you energy (especially fresh food).

- **Avoid indulging.** Skip all fatty and sugary snacks and focus on vegetables and other healthy options. Forget afternoon coffee with a bun, as it won't help you. Keep your weight and body fat within the recommended limits.

- **Get regular exercise.** The recommendation is at least half an hour of brisk exercise a day. A total of three hours or more of exercise per week is recommended.

- **Do not smoke or use tobacco, snuff, drugs**, energy drinks, coffee, black tea, or other addictive substances. They will do you no good in the long run.

- **Don't binge drink.** Alcohol kills brain cells and causes a hangover, which wastes time. However, some studies suggest that a glass of medium beer while socializing or a glass of wine with a meal can help lower blood pressure and improve social interaction.

- **Pray and meditate daily.** This will help to balance both blood pressure and stress.

- **Sleep eight hours a night**, as we said earlier.

- **Keep a positive attitude** towards life, as it adds years to your life and quality of life.

What to eat?

We have already covered the impact of physical activity on physical and mental health. Another critical area is nutrition. Finnish food has traditionally been healthy and nutritious, but of course, in recent decades, there has been an increasing shift towards industrial and processed (i.e., industrially processed) food in Finland, too. This development is also visible in Finland *as an Americanization of the waistline,* as processed food contains not only chemicals (marked with E-codes) but also considerably more fat, sugar, and other unhealthy ingredients, such as wheat flour, than homemade food. No diet is necessarily better than another, and many are harmful to health.

Here are some general dietary recommendations:

- Do not eat or drink more than the average amount. So, moderation in everything.

- Eat breakfast, lunch, snack, and dinner at regular intervals.

- Avoid all extreme and challenging diets.

- The secret to weight management is simple: eat fewer calories than you consume, and the weight will automatically fall over time (rapid weight loss is unhealthy, so there's no point in fooling yourself).

- Eat a balanced amount of carbohydrates, protein, and good fats.

- Go for wholegrain, organic, and other natural alternatives.

- Avoid processed foods and avoid foods with E-code ingredients.

A healthy diet is a holistic approach where everyday choices make a difference in the long term. Forget all the *'lose 20 pounds in a month'* programs because even if you achieve results, you will do so at the expense of your health. Changing your eating habits to healthy and balanced ones is better than bringing your weight back to normal. Abstinence from eating is also not an option, as our bodies need enough nutrients and energy to keep functioning. When there is a balance between energy intake and energy expenditure and energy comes from suitable sources, the weight will also remain stable in the long term.

In general, good sources of energy are protein, carbohydrates, and soft fats. To ensure that you get the essential nutrients and have a varied diet, you should ensure that the basics are in place and that everything is in moderation. All vegetables and wholegrain cereals are suitable as a staple for every meal and snack. Main meals and snacks, if needed, can be supported by low-fat and low-sugar oat milk products and a portion of pulses, tofu, seitan, fish, or meat (if you insist). Vegetable oils are suitable for cooking and salad dressings, and soft margarine is ideal for bread. Today, reducing the consumption of meat products is a good choice both for your health and for the environment.

High-quality sources of carbohydrates include whole grains, vegetables, mushrooms, roots, berries, fruits, nuts, and seeds, as they are rich in dietary fiber, vitamins, minerals, and other protective nutrients. However, processed or refined grains, such as products made from wheat flour, baked goods, sugar, rice, and white pasta, should be avoided as much as possible or replaced with more fiber-rich alternatives (e.g., whole meal options). The best energy sources for protein include dark green vegetables (such as spinach and pulses), fish, poultry, eggs, and nuts. Use red meat as little as possible, and avoid bacon and other processed meat products (such as sausages and ham). I know this is a tough pill for us to swallow (so look for healthier alternatives to replace these unhealthy current choices). But it is the price of health (no wonder there is so much cancer in the world today when we poison our bodies daily). Unfortunately, today's processed food is so industrialized that selling it in the grocery store is getting very close to misleading marketing.

There are three main problems with processed food: unhealthy additives, the amount and quality of sugar and fat. Healthy fats are soft. Vegetable oils, nuts, and seeds containing this type of fat are the best sources of fat for health (fish is also high in omega-3 fatty acids but is not an ethical choice). Avoid hard fats from foods containing butter, red meat, dairy products, cheese, or baked goods.

I'm all for easy ways to make life healthier and safer. One way to use quick insights to inform your food choices is to understand the labels on all the food you buy well. I used to read everything on product labels until I learned that you only need to check a few specific things on them, and then I knew that the product in question was closer to healthy than unhealthy. One rule on this checklist: if a product contains any of these ingredients at all or more than the appropriate level, I don't buy it; I look for a similar product with the correct values. The amounts on the list are per 3.5 ounces of product:

- *Energy in kilocalories (kcal):* an adult's typical daily energy requirement is around 2,000-3,000 kilocalories. The more calories a product contains, the less you can eat of it and other products. I roughly calculate how many calories I have eaten to ensure I am eating the right amount. I recommend skipping 400 kcal/3.5 ounces or more products, as they will quickly eat up your daily calorie quota.

- *Fat:* Aim for products that contain 0.2 ounces or less of total fat per 3.5 ounces.

- *Saturated fat:* this can quickly raise your cholesterol. I always recommend checking this figure and avoiding products that contain more than 0.2 ounces of saturated fat per 3.5 ounces.

- *Sugars:* avoid products containing more than 0.4 ounces of sugar per 3.5 ounces of product. If the product includes fresh fruit (such as orange juice), then 20g is still acceptable (but then limit how much you consume).

- *Fiber:* The product should contain 0.2 ounces or more of fiber.

- *Salt:* If salt is indicated as Sodium or Sodium, prefer products with 300 mg or less of Sodium or Sodium. If salt is a percentage, prefer products with less than 1% salt.

- *Not a single E-code substance.*

Also, be careful not to fall into these widespread traps in product labeling:

- ***Less fat*** does not mean that there is still not a lot of fat left in the product. There may just be a little less than before. Also, some low-fat products contain significantly more sugar than normal-fat products.

- ***Cholesterol-free*** does not necessarily mean that the product is not high in fat. Cholesterol is only present in animal-based products. For example, olive oil has no cholesterol, even though it is 100% fat.

- ***A light or diet*** label on a product does not necessarily mean anything. Always check the product's fat and sugar content per 100g using the guidelines above. In marketers' minds, a product may be light for any reason, perhaps because of its color, taste, or excitement. This also usually means that the product is artificially sweetened, which can be identified by the E-codes.

- ***No added sugar*** does not necessarily mean the product is low in sugar. It can only mean that no processed sugar has been added. Orange juice is an excellent example of this. It is better to look at the sugar content on the label and adjust the amount of sugar you consume accordingly.

- ***A fat-free*** product usually contains a lot of sugar or artificial sweeteners.

I went to the grocery store one day and started to crave juice. We don't usually drink juice because industrial juices don't contain any nutrients, so there is no reason to consume them. But sometimes, you can indulge your cravings, as long as it's the exception rather than the rule. So, I started going through the long shelf of juices on the list above in a huge grocery store. After looking through more than 20 juice cans, I still hadn't found one with less sugar than I wanted to consume. Even the juices with extensive text on the side saying *"contains less added sugar"* or *"no added sugar"* were still very sugary. Of course, this can be explained by the sugar in the fruit. Ultimately, I left the store without juice because none of the juices came in below the amount of sugar I wanted. Instead,

I decided to buy oranges, apples, and a couple of pears and eat them as they were (they gave me the juice I wanted and other benefits). Of course, another option would have been to take the juice and drink less of it; sometimes, I do that, too. The main idea of this example was that you don't have to be a total abstainer; you can make an informed decision based on what is important to you. Foods and drinks with a low glycemic index (i.e., low sugar) help the brain to function better, especially in the areas of willpower and self-discipline (which we will discuss much more about later in this book). Research has also shown that these foods help with weight management (and, in women, improve menstrual cycles):

- Most fruits, vegetables, and root vegetables are eaten as they are

- Cold-pressed juices from fruits, vegetables, and root vegetables

- Nuts and seeds

- Olive oil

We've covered the basics of the benefits of proper exercise and nutrition to help you achieve your goals. Depending on where you are now, some of these things may require significant changes to your current lifestyle. We'll look in more detail later at what you can do to form new habits. You don't have to change everything all at once, but you can listen to yourself to see the proper steps to change things and get concrete results, one step at a time. The benefits of developing your lifestyle are significant. We will now move on to the topic of financial health.

Create the economic conditions you want

Have you ever wondered why so many people don't have much money to spend when they retire? Or why do so many people have to work until they are old to put food on the table? The most common explanations are that they didn't earn enough at work, had a big family, had recessions, went bankrupt, etc. But I have yet to hear many people say that *I didn't care for my finances well enough*. It's amazing how less than 20% of adults have no savings. And it's easy to end up that way if you have neither an interest in self-discipline nor an interest in curbing your cravings. Today's world is all about spending, and savers are considered nihilists. I often feel like buying all sorts of nice things, such as a more excellent car, sports equipment, and toys for the big boys (I am ashamed to admit that I once bought a big remote-controlled helicopter, which cost me a lot of money and I never learned to fly it properly because it was not important enough to me in terms of time management). When you combine the above mindset with easy access to high-interest loans (over 3%), you don't need to check your savings account balance. In Finland, at least for some generations, children were still taught to save. They had nice-looking piggy banks (e.g., Scrooge McDuck sitting on a treasure chest) to put coins in, and then it was nice to take them to the bank and have the account balance visible in a jeans-covered bank book. Nowadays it's good if you don't have to pay to take your savings to the bank! Interest rates are so low that inflation is eating away at the money in the account. So many enjoy life here and now and worry about retirement later. However, that is a costly mistake. God willing, and you live until your retirement, it would be nice to live on a little more than a few hundred dollars a month and queue at the

> *Money is a tool, not a measure of your value. It reflects your creativity and focus on adding value to others and yourself.*

breadline, wouldn't it? But it's everyone's choice how to spend their income.

One of the book's principles is that *saving today is tomorrow's pleasure*. Short-sightedness is not the way to outdo yourself, achieve your goals, and make a living simultaneously. It requires more careful planning and holistic life management. Perhaps that's why so few people realize themselves at the level they could. What about you? Are you taking action, stepping up, and doing what it takes to be your fully capable self? ***That is your decision.***

Psychologically, we need to change the way we think about money. Instead of focusing on financial matters outside our Circle of Influence (more on this in a bit), such as the global economy, we need to focus on those things we can directly influence, such as saving and investing. Typically, people are triggered to spend when they get money; we want to trigger the urge to save. For us, satisfaction comes from responsible financial management, which involves saving and investing in the right proportions, not spending. Our enjoyment comes not from an expensive car that we buy with consumer credit but from a vehicle that we buy with cash at a price that fits our finances. We don't need the latest fashionable clothes (except in limited quantities if they take us towards our goals, for example, for work) or any other trinkets the world is running after. When a paycheck comes in, the first thing we always do is put a lump sum aside. Your goal should be to save at least 15-20% of your monthly net income (thus increasing the amount of dollars you save as your income increases). I save around 50-60% of my monthly income, as one of my long-term goals is to retire financially free by the age of 55. You cannot become financially free by working a traditional day job, so you must approach it differently.

How much do you currently save each month?

I save __________ percent of my income.

Saving as a term can already feel annoying (like you're missing out), so it's better to consider it a freedom fund. The money you save is an investment in your freedom, as it can allow you to choose where you spend your time financially. When you are economically free, you can go to work if you want, but it is not compulsory. This idea makes the seemingly forced choice of saving and momentary pleasure less desirable than investing in a freedom fund. Generally speaking, people save too little; even the 20% of people who have savings in general often have not saved above the so-called critical threshold. This is the limit at which you have invested enough money to pay your basic expenses with interest earned on your investments. And this limit depends on the lifestyle you want for yourself and your family. How much money do you think you should have invested to be financially free? Write the figure below because we'll soon calculate how much it is.

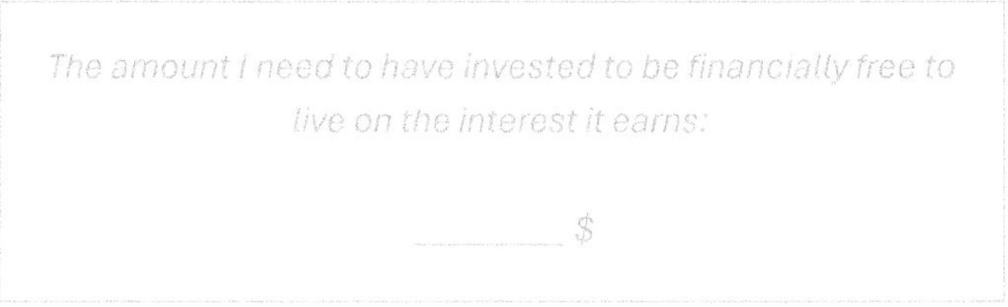

The most important advice I can give you, based on the teachings of the world's greatest billionaires (such as Warren Buffett and Bill Gates), is that you must commit to investing a fixed percentage of your income each month (regardless of its source) and you must do this the first time you receive the money. This way, you diversify your risk in the investment market and earn interest on the interest (we'll go through these in more detail). Before we get into the details of how to grow your finances, consider your savings rate. What percentage of your income do you commit to investing monthly whenever you receive an income?

_____ %

This figure is now your minimum investment figure. It goes on your monthly salary, Christmas and birthday presents, and unforeseen windfall income (such as an inheritance, bonus, or tax refund). This is your investment in your financial freedom.

Let's imagine you had started saving and investing earlier. According to the Stock Exchange Foundation, between 1994 and 2019, you would have received a return of around 10% on equities, around 5% on the government benchmark index, and around 2.5% on the money market index. According to the Findicator, apartments prices in Finland increased by 30% between the 1990s and 2017. All this time, these investments would have given you free money in your freedom fund if only you had invested it at the time. So, the most essential and first investment decision is how much money you put aside for your financial freedom.

Think about how often you go to restaurants or eat out weekly. Let's say you spend $40 a week on eating out and drinking coffee when you could save that without making significant lifestyle changes (take a coffee in a thermos or stop drinking coffee altogether). It may not seem like a lot, but what do you think $40 could be worth in the long run if you invested it instead of spending it? Assuming an annual return of 8% and leaving that money to grow for 40 years, the interest-on-interest principle turns that small $40 a week into half a million! What if you could save a hundred a month? That would make over a million at the same time.

Next, you need to automate your savings. It's easy with today's online banks: log in and set this amount to go automatically from your account on payday to your investment (we'll go through the options in more detail in a moment). You can invest in shares, index funds, pensions, and housing with just a few clicks. When this happens automatically, you don't have to think about what to invest, how much, or whether you can afford it. Your spending will be shaped by how much money you have: consider whether you're still spending as little money per month now as you did five years ago. Both your income and your expenses have likely increased. So, pay yourself first and then pay others. This is the most crucial investment decision you will make because if you have nothing *to* invest in, it doesn't matter *where* you invest.

Now that you have money to invest, we can focus on what's worth investing.[*] First, you can forget about taking advice from popular financial blog sites. There is no such thing as a sure-fire *"become a millionaire in six months"* program (although it is possible to make a million in six months). *Playing the lottery is not a strategy for wealth creation.* Nor does a five-star mutual fund guarantee you a return. Investment advisers who try to outsmart the market may be successful in the short term, but their performance usually does not last (96% of funds return less than the general market would allow). Who or what can you rely on for income?

Diversification across different investment instruments and markets, the interest-for-interest principle, and the return on low-cost, long-term indices. The key is to plan and keep a cool head when the market is choppy. Warren Buffet (one of the world's wealthiest people) was so sure that even the best stock advisors could not beat passive index investing that he made a million-dollar bet with them in 2008. The aim was to see which would do better, his passive S&P500 index investment or the active funds. 2019 Warren was declared the winner (and he still expects to get his million from the losing stock advisors). Warren's strategy is not to try to outsmart the market but to follow it and automatically invest according to each market situation. This makes investing cheaper in terms of costs and more manageable in execution. Above all, it generates more profit by collecting profits from the market

---

[*] Although I have a PhD from the Turku School of Economics, I am not a professional investment adviser, and I am not giving you any investment advice. Everything in this book is just a suggestion and has worked very well for me and many others, but you must make your own decisions. If you are not sure, then seek advice from officially regulated investment advisers (do not use informal investment advisers at all).

according to what happens there, rather than trying to beat the market and guess which way each stock will go. According to a Vanguard study, between 1984 and 1998, only eight out of 200 funds outperformed the S&P500 index in America.

One of the worst potential problems with investing that banks don't want you to know about is the impact of expenses on the return on your investment. Banks profit billions of dollars a year from their clients' investment costs. And because many don't understand the impact of costs on their investment returns, few spend the time researching them to optimize returns. Even a small difference in costs has a huge impact on total returns. For calculation purposes, imagine you have a nice round figure invested: a million dollars. Let's say you invest it in a fund for 30 years and get an average annual return of 8%. Here are three different expense levels for that fund: 1%, 2%, and 3%. Before you look at the answer below, guess how many millions the difference in the final return is between the 1% and 3% cost of the fund. Here are the income statements:

- 1%: $ 7,6 million

- 2%: $ 5,7 million

- 3%: $ 4,3 million

All other data remained the same in this example except for the fund's expenses. So, a fund with only a 1% cost will generate 3.3 million, or 57% more than a fund with a 3% cost! This is due to the money wasted on expenses over the years, and thus the lower interest rate to interest effect. Has it *ever occurred to you that the cost of the funds you use dramatically impacts how much money you end up with?* For me, at least, this calculation came as a surprise when I first saw it from Anthony Robbins. I immediately went to check the costs of all the funds I was using, and to my dismay, I found that most of them were taking more than 2% out of my expenses, the worst even more than 4%. Today, I would not even consider a fund that charges such high costs because I do not want more than half of the profit to go to the bank and less to me. If you already have funds in place, I recommend that you check their charges immediately. And if you don't have any funds yet, keep reading and avoid this mistake in the future.

Financial freedom is the dream of many, but few people consciously try to achieve it. And perhaps a big reason for this is that it seems significant and challenging to achieve in the current life situation. In such a mindset, the goal is one large sum, which seems almost impossible. But perhaps you will be comforted to know that there are five figures for financial freedom, not just one big one! It's also possible that two or three of these figures are enough for you, and you don't want to reach the top level of total financial freedom. So, what are these five levels of financial freedom?

1. Economic Security

2. Financial Success

3. Financial independence

4. Economic freedom

5. Comprehensive economic freedom

I'll review these five levels to help you decide the most suitable. For some, even the lowest level of financial security is enough (although I count on God for my security instead of money, there's no harm in a nest egg and wise financial practices). Few of us get total financial freedom, so these are all milestones on the journey. You can choose which levels are most appropriate for you over five years, which ten, and which twenty. This will give you a financial map to help you navigate your way there. Of course, you can also play the lottery and hope for the best (I once got six number matches in the lottery and about ten grand, but I don't even know where that money is now, which is a bit sad).

Economic security

Let's start with the first level, financial security (although the only absolute security is in the Lord). This means enough passive income (i.e., money that you don't have to go to work in the morning for) to cover basic expenses:

- Mortgage loan

- Property costs (electricity, water, heating, rent)

- Home cooking

- Basic travel expenses (essential car or public transport)

- Basic insurance (home, car, health)

- Telecommunications

If you could pay all the above expenses without going to work, would that be enough financial freedom for you? I think many people would say yes, and this was the first level of financial freedom I sought. People spend, on average, about:

- 11 500 $ for housing

- 4 400 $ for food

- 5 800 $ for basic travel expenses

- 900 $ for telecommunications

For example, the average annual consumption expenditure is around $ 37,000 (including more than the items listed above). But do you know how much this amount would be for you?

Mortgage loan: _______________ $ per month

Property costs:	_________ $ per month
Food:	_________ $ per month
Basic travel expenses:	_________ $ per month
Basic insurance:	_________ $ per month
Telecommunications:	_________ $ per month
IN TOTAL PER MONTH:	_________ $ per month
TOTAL PER YEAR: Monthly cost times 12 =	_________ $ per year

This is the first level of economic freedom to strive for!

The next interesting question is how much money you must invest to achieve this financial security level. Many different calculators are online, but I will use the free savings calculator from a bank website this time. Let's assume that your amount was $ 22,600 per year. Assuming a 10-year savings period and an annual return of 6.1%, the calculator shows us... $ 280,000! So, for the price of one detached house, you could make yourself financially secure in this example. For many people, and perhaps for you too, saving that amount is possible, especially if you use the principle of interest on interest (knowing that over the last ten years, the real return on equities has been around 6%). So, fill in the table above with your figures and use the online return calculators to see how much you should have invested and write the figure below:

My financial security investment amount is:
_________ $

In addition to the above amount, you should also have a so-called *rainy day fund*. This is money in an easily accessible place for major life upheavals (remember that if you start spending money from the financial freedom fund, your freedom will run out very quickly, and any money you put in there should stay there). But because life happens unexpectedly, you should save at least six months' worth of expenses, but preferably 12 months' worth in an emergency fund that you can use if you need it (like a job loss).

Financial success

The next level is the financial performance fund. This includes financial security and other basic luxuries (such as gym, clothing, and leisure). Calculating this is now a little easier once you have already calculated the annual cost of the security level:

Financial security	_________	$ per month
(from a previous calculation)		
Clothing costs:	_________	$ per month
Leisure:	_________	$ per month
Fitness and health:	_________	$ per month
IN TOTAL PER MONTH:	_________	$ per month
TOTAL PER YEAR:		
Monthly cost times 12 =	_________	$ per year

This is the second most desirable level of economic success cost per year! People spend, on average, $ 1,000 a year on clothes, $ 1,200 on health, and $ 3,500 on leisure. If we add these to the $ 22,600 in the previous example, we get a total of $ 28,300 for the example calculation.

You can now use the same return calculator and assumptions as before and calculate how much your financial success is worth. In the above example, you must invest around $350,000 to achieve financial success.

My financial success is the amount invested in:

_____________ $

Financial independence

The third level of economic freedom is economic independence. At this level, for the first time, it can be said that one's time no longer must be dedicated to work. At the level of economic independence, all your essential expenses are covered by passive income. How much money do you need per year for your expenses? You can use the information you have collected in this calculation and add the remaining costs. Only you know exactly what to add to this list. Below is an example from Statistics Finland of what you can include in the calculation. There are also a few blank lines where you can write in any other expenses you want to include in your financial independence (remember, however, that at this level, it is not yet a matter of total financial independence):

Financial success _____________ *$ per month*
(from a previous calculation)

All travel expenses: _____________ *$ per month*

All insurances: _____________ *$ per month*

Alcohol, snus, and tobacco: _____________ *$ per month*
(I recommend you avoid this expenditure altogether)

Furnishing and household appliances: _____________ *$ per month*

This is the third most desirable cost of economic independence per year! Statistics Finland shows Finns's average total consumption expenditure is around $ 37,500 per year.

Once again, you can use the same calculator and assumptions as before and calculate how much your financial independence investment amount is. In the above example, you only need to invest around $480,000 to succeed financially. With just under half a million, you could already be financially independent!

Does this amount of financial independence still seem as impossible to you as before? Of course, your expenses may be higher than the average for Finns. In this case, you should review your costs and consider how to reduce them. My amount for financial independence requires an investment of around $ 700,000, based on the assumptions above. The exciting thing about low-cost, interest-on-interest investments is that although the value of the investment can fluctuate wildly over the years, the figure rises steadily upwards over the long term. Suppose you couldn't find a suitable return calculator online to get the above statistics. In that case, you can use an easy trick: assume that your investment returns 5% per year, and thus, you can calculate the amount you need to invest by multiplying your annual expenses by 20 (as we discussed earlier investment expenses and found that a 1% difference in costs had a significant impact on the return on investment, the same is valid for investment returns. A 1% difference in the calculation will increase the amount of money you need to invest significantly).

How do these first three levels of economic freedom sound to you? Do they feel like if you could get your investment to this level, you could free yourself to pursue the dreams this book will help you achieve? Do you want to see yourself financially independent? For most of us, this would be a life-changing situation where we could free ourselves from the enforced slavery of work (you have to do something with your life anyway, so it might be work, but of your own free will).

Economic freedom

The next and slightly more challenging level is economic freedom. This level includes all your current living expenses plus a few luxuries. What would be the most uplifting spending items you want to keep in a state of financial freedom? Perhaps your thing is to donate money to the church? Or do you want a convertible for hot summer days or a fishing boat for a summer cottage? For many Finns, the summer cottage itself is already a highly desirable item of expenditure, so perhaps it's on your list of financial freedom? Please choose one or two of the most essential things, calculate how much they would cost you monthly, and add them to the annual cost of financial independence calculated above.

Financial independence _________ $ per month
(from a previous calculation)

Additional purchase #1:
______________________ $ per month

Additional purchase #2:
______________________ $ per month

Additional purchase #3:
______________________ $ per month

IN TOTAL PER MONTH: _________ $ per month

TOTAL PER YEAR:
Monthly cost times 12 = _________ $ per year

This is the fourth most desirable cost of economic freedom per year! *Once* again, you can use the same calculator and assumptions as before to work out how much your financial freedom investment will be.

My financial freedom investment amount is:

_________ $

For example, my financial freedom investment is around $1.4 million. This includes the needs of a family of three, five trips abroad a year, and a couple of cars.

Comprehensive economic freedom

Next, total financial freedom is the highest level you can aspire to and takes the most effort to reach. You can afford everything you need and the desired luxuries at this level. We have burned this image into our retinas when dreaming of winning the lottery. And what could be better if you happen to get the seven numbers you need the right (although it's worth bearing in mind that, according to the National Lottery's website, there are 15 380 937 different lottery lines. Calculating this gives a probability of winning the lottery of 1/15 380 937 = 0.0000065%). The number is a bit hard to understand without context, so let's look at other exciting probabilities that are significantly better than winning the lottery[*]:

- You have about a 1 / 39 000 = 0.002% chance of getting into one of the best universities in the world.

- You are more likely to be eaten by a shark on your Thailand holiday, which could be 1 / 11 500 000 = 0.000008 %.

- To be one of the most intelligent people in the world, let's say, getting an IQ score of over 180 on a Mensa test. This is possible with a 1 / 3 500 000 = 0.00002% probability.

- Let's say you want to have four children at one time. Even that is more likely than winning the lottery! 1 / 13 000 000 = 0.000006% to be exact.

- The probability of being struck by lightning is about 1 / 1 000 000 = 0.0001%. Much more (un)lucky than winning the lottery!

- How about playing golf? It makes much more sense than playing the lottery since a hole-in-one has a 1/12,000 = 0.008% chance of hitting the hole for an amateur player. If you get into golf and play it once a week, you can hit the hole once every 13 years. Or if bowling is more your thing, you're just as likely to play a perfect 300. The same can't be said for winning the lottery, even if you play it once a week for the rest of your life.

We could go on with the list above for considerably longer, but perhaps the idea is starting to become apparent. The lottery is not a strategy for

---

[*] https://www.fool.com/slideshow/25-things-more-likely-happen-you-winning-lottery/?slide=1

wealth creation. Indeed, the most significant difference between rich and poor is that the rich do more of the right things, and they learn and improve as they develop their wealth. Consider the American Les Brown, who has become a billionaire despite being born into a broken, alcoholic household with no money even for food. This forced Les first to figure out how to get food (and money for it) and then how to get enough for the whole family. And he continued that path at a time when black men, in general, didn't have much opportunity in America. Everyone comes from somewhere, and the best place to start is right where you are. But remember what Albert Einstein said: "*It is useless to expect different results if you keep doing the same things repeatedly.*" New results require new perspectives.

From an economic mathematical point of view, we continue the same path as in the previous example of economic freedom. Add on top of that the dreams of your life that you want to have total financial freedom. Perhaps it involves a sailboat, a holiday home abroad, or something lovely. Again, calculate the cost of these per month and year and add it to the previous financial freedom total. What is your level 5 figure?

Economic freedom *(from a previous calculation)*	__________ *$ per month*
Dream #1: _______________________	*$ per month*
Dream #2: _______________________	*$ per month*
Dream #3: _______________________	*$ per month*
IN TOTAL PER MONTH:	__________ *$ per month*

***This is the fifth most desirable cost of overall economic freedom per
year! Once*** again, you can use the same calculator and assumptions as
before and calculate how much your total financial freedom investment
will be.

You may recall that I mentioned at the beginning of this chapter that
you do not have to aim for all five levels but can settle for any of them
(even the first level is a significant improvement for most of us). My
ambitions in this area end at level 4, and I have no grand dreams of
further advancement. For me, the things more essential than money are
family, friends, charity, and following Jesus. I know that if I set myself
a goal of total financial freedom, not only will I get there, but I will also
have to cut back on more important things because of time constraints.

Now that you know all your readings and understand their financial
and life-management implications, you can write a summary of them
here:

Annual target _____________ $

Amount invested _____________ $

Financial independence

Annual target _____________ $

Amount invested _____________ $

Economic freedom

Annual target _____________ $

Amount to be invested _____________ $

Comprehensive financial freedom

Annual target _____________ $

Amount invested _____________ $

In practice, you can be rich by having more than you need or needing less. So far, we've gone through your financial aspirations in concrete numbers. This is important because a clear goal is much easier than a vague dream. Next, we'll examine your action plan to reach these goals.

From thought to financial action

The first step is straightforward, but for many, it is complex: *save more and invest better*. The more you can save, the more you can invest, and the faster you can reach your financial goals. Many people have told me they'd rather spend and enjoy today than save for tomorrow because they don't know if they'll live until then. And so what? They don't have financial freedom as a goal; everyone has to choose a lifestyle that suits them. I save about 50-60% of my monthly net income automatically, but you already know your savings figure based on the exercises you've gone through in the past. There are countless savings tips on the internet, and hundreds of books have been written. But many of these require too much willpower. That's why I prefer a simple approach: automatically transferring a certain percentage of my monthly income into a savings account, investments, a mortgage, and a rainy-day fund. That way, I no longer have to think about it, and I can adjust my end-of-month spending according to the money I have left.

To save more, you need to change your mindset about spending and consider which is more critical: ego-shopping or financial freedom. For example, consider the following:

- How much do you need to spend on clothes, shoes, jewelry, etc., or can you spend more and longer on what you already have? This will save you money and the environment significantly, as clothing is the single most significant contributor to CO_2 emissions in individual people's lives.

- Need the latest model and the giant TV and stereo? If you don't make your viewing experience too comfortable, you'll save time and money.

- Does your car need to be bigger and nicer than your neighbors and colleagues? Cars are a significant expense, not only in terms of purchase price but also in terms of maintenance, fuel, and wearing parts.

- Is an excellent daily *frappalappacino coffee* and a bun necessary, or do you save even a tenner and drink your coffee for free at work or cheap at home? That's how you save calories as well as money.

- If you have to consider buying something in installments, do you need it? The interest in hire purchase will eat up your funds very quickly. I have never bought anything on hire purchase because of this (apart from a few things bought at 0% interest to let my money produce as long as possible before it goes out).

These are moments when you have to think about which way of spending money gives you more satisfaction, the consumer or the leisure economy. The table below will help you to define this in practical terms. On the left-hand side, please write down your most common purchases and estimate how much they cost you and how much they give you pleasure. Then, in the last column, you can also estimate what you want to do with each expense in the future (for example, whether you will continue to spend or stop spending):

Cost	Cost $ per time/day	Cost $ per month	Provides pleasure 0-10*	What do I do with the cost in the future?

TOTAL:

** 0 = No pleasure at all and 10 = Gives a great feeling.*

In the table above, fill in at least six of your most common expenses not part of your mandatory living costs (we went through these earlier). In particular, think about the last column for each expense. ***Could you give up some of these expenses for your financial freedom?***

The next step is to understand your bank charges. I mentioned earlier that investment costs significantly impact returns even at low percentage differences. Ensure that all your banking is based on the lowest costs available. Go through all your bank charges and make them competitive:

- Costs of day-to-day management.

- Bank and credit card charges.

- ♦ Loan charges and interest: always compare the total interest rate (APR) to consumer protection law.

- ♦ Mortgage costs: ensure you always have the cheapest loan on the market.

- ♦ Investment expenses.

Always aim to pay the highest interest rate on your loan first. If you have any high-interest consumer loans, pay them off first. If you have a mortgage, pay it off as quickly as possible (make sure you have a loan that you can pay off faster for free). If you have extra money somewhere, always pay off the most expensive money first and invest the rest.

The third step to increasing wealth is personal financial management. Few want to start managing their finances like a business accountant, but simple expense planning and management are helpful. It brings transparency and insight into where the money is going, not just where we think it is going. I use the free Buxfer* software, which allows you to track your expenses and income, manage your budget, and calculate your net worth. All you have to do on the site is upload your bank statements once a month, and the system does the rest. The primary purpose of expense management is to decide in advance where and how much money you will spend. This helps to avoid impulse purchases. In addition to budget management, I use automated price-tracking sites. If I've decided to buy something important (like a Garmin Fenix 6 Pro Sapphire watch for sports), I turn on automatic price trackers from different websites (like price-tracking.com) and use them to decide when it's the right time to buy the product. This way, I can ensure I get the best price on the market (at least at that moment) and minimize the money I spend. Of course, all this takes more effort than buying on impulse and not managing your finances, but this effort is rewarded quickly with increased financial freedom. Why bother? Think of the cappuccinos and other specialty coffees that people buy every day. Let's say a cup costs you about four dollars a day. What will that do to your

---

* https://www.buxfer.com/acceptInvite?e=6042a678db7499ce56ba6e450fca5c9c

lost economic freedom in 20 years? If we use a 6% interest rate as a basis for the calculation, these daily cups of coffee cost $ 56,500! How many people think in this perspective when queuing at the counter at Starbucks? Or why buy bottled water when you can drink from the tab? Fortunately, you and I know better and invest the money in our financial freedom.

The three themes above focused on saving money. Next, we will look at ideas on how to earn more. This is both an exciting and challenging topic. In short, *your earnings are directly proportional to what others will pay for the value you add.* So the essential question is: how can you make yourself and the value you add even more valuable to others? This requires understanding the needs of others and your ability to meet them. This is why it pays to invest in yourself so that your skills, knowledge, experience, and abilities grow and thus enable you to deliver more value. Anthony Robbins even goes so far as to urge us to work on self-development even more than our day jobs. He says that all we need to do to earn more in the same amount of time is to become more valuable to others. In a sense, this is also what the Bible says. It says that *whoever among you wants to become great, let him be your servant.* If the Bible is not your thing, the world's most excellent financial guru, Warren Buffett, has said that the best investment of his life was an investment in himself, and anyone can make that investment. How could you add value to others? Write down your thoughts in the box below:

Where can you find the economic turbo button?

We have already gone through some of the ideas related to investing. We still have a few essential topics left to help you move toward financial freedom more quickly. The first is investment allocation, the second is diversification, and the third is tax planning. Since tax planning depends on everyone's situation, I won't discuss it in depth in this book. However, I would like to give some guidance on three things to consider:

- Don't settle for an automatic tax bill sent to you by the government. Please read through all the essential information required on your tax form and understand what it means and how to use it.

- Make a tax plan for the next tax year in advance. Go through the changes for that year and make a plan for how you will make use of them during the year. File the necessary information and receipts carefully, as a tax audit is entirely possible (I've been through a tax audit twice myself, and the first time, I was missing one receipt for just over $7. The government claimed the money back from me, although I didn't have to pay it in the end as it was less than the $10 minimum).

- Prepare your tax bill in time; don't leave it to the last minute. You may need help with some things, and getting it for free is easier if you're not in a hurry. In addition, check the form several times before sending it, as you don't want to leave any incorrect information (which can easily lead to a tax audit and penalty).

Let's go back to the distribution of investments. This is a critical topic because the first important decision is to invest, and the next important decision is where to invest. You must establish a set of investment principles you will follow regardless of the market situation. This decision is far more critical than the objects you invest in, whether in housing, shares, or others. Both asset allocation and diversification are about reducing risk by keeping assets separate and splitting focuses on not investing in just one investment category, such as shares or housing. Conversely, diversification focuses on spreading your investments across different geographical areas to reduce risk. This works particularly well in crises in certain regions of the world (such as a recession in Finland or a tsunami in Asia). The coronavirus is a global event that caused a change in market conditions in all countries, especially in equities. In such a situation, geographical diversification does not help because shares lose value everywhere. But in such a situation, diversification is beneficial because, for example, housing did not fall as quickly and as much, and the price of gold even rose. So, combining the two techniques ensures that even if some of your investments temporarily do not perform, the fall in value is balanced by allocating your investments to different themes and diversifying across different areas. *You should not put all your eggs in the same basket because they will all fall apart if the basket drops.* And if all this sounds a bit tricky, you're right. Fortunately, by applying the *"quick fix"* principle in this book, we can find easy ways to achieve the same result without becoming investment experts. And because reading the financial markets is extremely difficult even for the best professionals in the field, we don't have a great chance of success. Take housing, for example. Most would say yes if you ask professionals whether buying a house makes sense. But if you purchased a home around 2006, you'd almost certainly regret your decision around 2008, when prices plummeted after the mortgage bubble burst. *Investment problems often arise when good people do the right things at the wrong time.* If you bought shares in late 2019, you'll probably regret it in early 2020, when the interest rate virus temporarily crashed the stock market. You could have bought twice as many shares for the same money a few months later. Sure, the value of your investment would have increased if you had held on to the shares until at least 2022. This is where dividing investments into different categories reduces risk and helps us ordinary people. When the value of one goes down (e.g., stocks during a rate hike), another can go up (e.g., gold at the same time). So, we divide our investments into two different types: safe and yield-seeking. Safe investments don't increase value much, but they don't lose it quickly. Yield investments, on the other hand, can fluctuate a lot in value over the long term, but they also allow for more significant growth. So how much should you invest in each? This depends on how long you must wait for your investments to grow and how much risk you are prepared to take. As a rule of thumb, you should not have anything in income investments you are unprepared to lose.

As this book is not an investment guide, I cannot go into depth on the different investing methods in each investment category. However, I will list some common ways to invest more safely and profitably. I recommend contacting a regulated investment adviser to review the non-options and plan what works best for you.

The safest investments (although they all have their risks) are:

- Own home and summer cottage/real estate
- Cash/money/savings accounts and other bank deposits
- Debentures and bonds
- Life and health insurance
- Fixed income investments
- Pension

Income-oriented investments, on the other hand, include:

- Shares
- Indices and investment funds (active and passive)
- Foreign exchange investments
- Antiques and collectables
- Other loans

Investment diversification is an additional layer on top of investment classes, as it spreads investments across different areas within an investment class. Diversification within each asset class reduces the risks associated with individual countries, companies, or sectors. Diversification within an asset class is essential for equity investments. In addition to diversification of investments, diversification over time is also crucial, especially when starting to invest and when investing more significant amounts. Over the long term, an investor has a positive return expectation, regardless of when they start. Therefore, the best time to start investing is now. However, be aware that in the short term, there is a risk of being bought at the top of the market, and it can take years to recover from a fall (as has happened to many people who invested in equities just before the interest rate boom). When investing large lump sums such as gifts, inheritance, business profits, or savings accumulated in a savings account, it is advisable to split the investment into several small parts, which can then be invested in the market over 1-3 years. In typical situations, however, regular, automated savings is the easiest way to spread investments over time. By investing in equal amounts each month, you can buy in both booms and busts, so you get more shares in a down market and less in a boom market.

As a result of diversification and allocation between asset classes, the value of your investments will change over time as some investments rise and others fall. This leads to an imbalance where your actual portfolio does not match your planned allocation. For example, when the stock market increases significantly, without rebalancing the portfolio, an investor could end up with 40-50% of assets in equities instead of the planned 30%. Naturally, finding the right balance for yourself regarding diversification would be best. The table below can give you some ideas for planning:

Type of investor	SO	AO	EO	MM	VL	YL	KI
Security-search	5 %	10%	10%	5%	25%	20%	10%
Neutral	10%	15%	15%	10%	15%	15%	10%
For profit	15%	20%	20%	15%	10%	5%	10%
Resistant to wobbles	10%	10%	10%	Gold 10%	35%	15%	10%

In the table above: SO = National equities, AO = American equities, EO = European equities, MM = Other markets, VL = Government loans, YL = Corporate loans, KI = Real estate

In normal market conditions, investors should review their diversification once a year. It is also worth considering the potential tax implications of this activity if the sale of certain investments results in a gain and, hence, capital taxes payable.

Am I right in thinking that, at this point, all the above is starting to seem quite complicated and a lot of work? And if you do it all yourself, that's what it is. I mentioned earlier that by applying the principle of *'quick thinking,'* help is available for this, too, which will bring similar returns without having to do it yourself. Don't worry; next time, there will be no snake oil advertising or secret tricks. Many investment service providers on the market understand the above principles very well and apply them to their funds. So, others will do the work for you, and you will avoid tax and other hassles! On the websites of banks and other investment service providers, you can find active funds with reasonable charges (less than 2%), and asset allocation and diversification are already considered. Such funds allocate a predefined percentage of their investments to security-seeking assets and the rest to income-seeking assets.

One of the services I use is Vanguard, and you can choose whether to put 20%, 40%, 60%, or 80% into income investing and the rest into safety investing automatically. The cost is just over 1%, which is acceptable considering that their active fund invests precisely how I want without worrying about it. The fund in question has returned around 13% for me in good times, and during the interest rate boom, it has dropped less than many of its peers (and was still in profit by around 3% for 2020 and 7% for 2021). However, I do not recommend this or any other fund; it is up to you to find a suitable solution (you can use a supervised investment adviser for this if you need to). Another option is to use passive index funds focusing on different markets. Examples include the S&P500 in America and the FTSE100 and FTSE250 in the UK. Finland has its own, as do Asia and other markets. These have charges of around

0.5% and track the largest companies in the market, automatically rebalancing the portfolio at specific intervals. If you invest in indices of this type in different markets, you again get automated diversification in the stock market (however, these do not help you with asset class allocation; you have to do it separately). The advantage of both options described above is that you will not incur any capital tax consequences for doing these portfolio rebalances because they are done automatically within the portfolios.

Time is money! Or is money time?

Let's recap the principles discussed in this chapter to help you increase your financial opportunities to meet your goals from an investment perspective:

- Plan and implement a sensible asset allocation for your investments (consider using a *volatility-proof* investment model). Don't put all your eggs in one basket.

- Diversify your investments across markets so that if one area goes down, another may not.

- Don't try to beat the market with your cunning, timing, or individual investments. Use regular investing that spreads your entry price evenly over a long time. Avoid significant lump-sum investments because of the risk they carry.

- Automate your investing as much as possible, using monthly transfers as soon as your salary comes in and taking advantage of low-cost, automatically self-balancing funds.

Initially, this chapter wasn't supposed to focus so heavily on investing. Still, when I weighed up both my results and the advice of the world's wealthiest people, it seemed like the most helpful direction for the goals of this book: *your financial liberation to pursue the most meaningful things in your life*, whatever they may be. However, there are many other ways to grow financially in the area you want to focus on. I can't go into everything in depth here because that would take up a book.

Here are a few suggestions that you can explore in more depth depending on your situation:

♦ Government project funding for various purposes.

♦ Adult learning support from the state.

♦ hundreds of foundations provide grants for various purposes every year. (For example, thanks to the Finnish Association of Information Writers, which has supported the production of this book.)

♦ Party and association subsidies, grants, subsidies, etc.

♦ Bank and other loans (but not including the effect of charges and interest).

♦ Selling your surplus goods, crafts, etc.

♦ Crowdfunding and sponsorship.

♦ Student grants, loans, wage subsidies, unemployment benefits, and social assistance.

♦ Government loans for businesses and start-ups and start-up money. Leader funding for local activities.

The above list is not exhaustive; you can find better places to get financial support for your activities. The main thing is to think about how you can achieve your goals in a sustainable financial way.

One way to measure what you should focus on in monetary terms is to use an hourly rate. You can get your hourly rate either directly from your pay slip (or contract) or by using this formula:

Annual salary divided by 1920 (40 hours a week times 48 working weeks a year). If you earn $50,000 per year, you will earn $26 per hour.

<table>
<tr><td>Annual salary</td><td>_________ $</td></tr>
<tr><td>Divided by 1920</td><td>_________ $ / h</td></tr>
</table>

Once you know your hourly rate, you can concentrate on doing only things worth at least that hourly rate or more. All other things you can, from a financial point of view, prioritize lower. Of course, this value doesn't work for prioritizing everything (for example, time with family). Still, in some situations, it can give you a different perspective, for example, when your neighbor Maija offers to work on sweeping her yard for ten an hour.

To summarize this chapter, here are ten principles for growing your wealth:

1. Define what wealth and financial freedom mean to you. How much wealth do you need to feel well-off or financially free?

2. Keep the bar you set above as your target; don't move it according to your current or future wealth. This is your base figure for wealth.

3. Make sure that the definition you set for your wealth is one that you think is possible.

4. Make a plan to get you there.

5. List all the reasons you want to achieve the level of wealth you have defined. Why is it important to you?

6. Refine your plan (for example, follow the instructions in this book).

7. Start implementing your plan immediately. Follow it up and develop it.

8. Be responsible for your results because no one else will be for you.

9. Don't give up when things get difficult; change your action plan until it works.

10. Run your finances like a business and monitor them with proper financial reports.

This chapter aims to give you the information you need to grow your financial freedom in the most passive way possible (of course, free lunches are not for everyone, so you'll have to put in some effort). Next, we can move on to self-development.

Ever more advanced you

We believe what we say about ourselves. We put into practice what we think about ourselves. And what we put into practice makes us who we are.

Good self-discipline and a focus on what matters most are needed to achieve sustainable results. I have read hundreds of non-fiction books, biographies, and guides, and most of them encourage people to spend their lives more purposefully and emphasize the importance of self-discipline. Some days, it's easier to get things done than others, but every day, it's worth focusing on doing the right things (more on that later). And it will be no surprise that this is not a one-off but an everyday challenge.

Willpower (an essential part of self-discipline) is a muscle, like the biceps, and can be strengthened. And just as the biceps get tired after a chin-up, willpower also wears down during the day and needs rest. An

American marriage counselor, Don Baucom, has fascinatingly described this. His advice to couples who work day jobs and fight at home in the evenings was to leave work early and spend more time together in the evenings. But wait a minute! After all, these couples fight at home in the evenings, so why should they spend even more time together? Don had noticed that people often exhaust their willpower during the workday, and every impulse starts to get on their nerves when they get home. If they went home when they had gas left in the willpower tank, they could focus on spending more quality time together. And this advice has been a marriage saver for thousands of couples. The important lesson is that we need to understand the amount of willpower we have and channel it into useful things. We should also develop our willpower by overcoming adversity one by one so (instead of all at once) that it stops consuming our willpower. For me, fitness is an excellent example of this. When I first started running, going out was very difficult some days. Now, a couple of years later, I go out the door for a run with a smile, and it doesn't take any willpower; it gives me energy. I have a new habit, which is the opposite of the one I had before. You can also change your thoughts, like indulging or exercising. Instead of struggling and using up your willpower, you can slowly change your actions to sneak into a new, healthier way of life without suffering!

One thing that comes up repeatedly in top performers' advice is the effect of training on willpower. The thing that unites both Navy Seals and world breath-holding champion David Blaine is that when the going gets tough (as it certainly does when you are surpassing both yourself and world records), they can rely on the experience of their training. This allows the soldier to remain calm and combat-ready even when bullets are passing through their limbs, and it will enable a person in a drowning state to hold their breath a little longer. David had spent thousands of hours practicing breath-holding in England in conditions he had defined himself (such as the river Thames in London). When he went on TV in America on Oprah to set a world record for breath-holding, he thought he was ready. But he soon discovered that the studio lighting, audience, the loud timer outside the glass pool, and many other conditions were more challenging than being in a cold and dirty river. Instead of dropping, his heart rate rose, and he consumed significantly more oxygen than he should have. The previous world record was 16:32 minutes, and by the ten-minute mark, David was already starting to lose feeling in his toes. A few minutes later, his heart rate started to behave erratically between 40 and 150 BPM when it should have stayed steady at around 50. At fifteen minutes, his heart started to skip a beat, and the compulsive need to breathe hit him. He let go of the rope that held him to the bottom and floated backward to the top of the pool. An ambulance and medical staff were on standby to resuscitate. David got out of the by himself and collapsed on the floor. And what happened? He beat the world record with a new time of 17 minutes and 4 seconds! David said afterward that his training helped him to know his reactions so well that he could stay in as long as possible. Thus, his last few minutes in the pool were not based on willpower but on experience. This same mindset works for us. By educating ourselves on new things and gaining a solid understanding of them, we don't need to fight with willpower. David says that *setting and achieving small goals will help you achieve bigger goals that you couldn't possibly achieve otherwise. He* goes on to say that *it's not just about practicing certain things but about making your life more challenging overall, and thus training yourself to be always prepared* to have a little bit in store, *no matter how challenging the situation.*

If you want to practice willpower, here are two exercises for you, both challenging and valuable. The first exercise is physical, and the second is mental. Both are simple but not necessarily easy.

Physical exercise involves sitting in a good, upright posture. This exercise is easy, especially when sitting at work or school. I'm doing it right now as I write this book. Good posture helps with back problems and makes you look more confident. In today's sedentary culture, lousy posture is prevalent, so good posture makes you stand out. Try sitting with a good posture until the end of this chapter. At one time, I first started keeping my posture consciously but found it took too much concentration away from my work. So, I got posture support to hold my shoulders back. It felt uncomfortable but didn't require me to do anything because I kept a good posture with support. Posture experts recommend avoiding posture supports precisely because they don't develop the muscles needed for good posture. I then searched online for solutions and found a product called *Upright Go 2*, a small white device attached to the back of the neck with skin tape and connected to a smartphone. The device monitors your posture and gives a small vibrating warning (like a vibrating phone alarm) if your posture goes terribly. This device has worked for me, at least, because it makes you hold your posture well by yourself. It develops the right muscles, but it doesn't require concentration. I know that the device will remind me if I slouch over time while sitting.

The second exercise is more mental: think about why and how you say everything you say. Here, you use your willpower to improve your communication. This is a challenging exercise because very few people are used to thinking about what they say beforehand. This is probably the case for you, as it is for me. But how much better would this world be if everyone thought about what they say and how it might affect others? This, if anything, requires the development of willpower.

Of course, in addition to developing willpower, an effective tactic is organizing things so that doing the right thing becomes as easy as possible and minimizing the temptation to do things wrong. However, it's best not to test your willpower too much because harmful consequences are usually immediate when it fails. Therefore, people with high willpower tend to try to be in as few situations where it is tested as possible. If every day is a struggle, self-discipline fails at some point.

Exercise and food are vital for the body, but the Holy Bible also says that *man does not live by bread alone but by every word that comes from the mouth of God* (Matthew 4:4). Even if you don't believe in God, read this anyway. Psychologist Michael McCullough (University of Miami), who unfortunately says he is not a believer, has studied the meaning of God in life and has found a robust scientific basis for faith. According to hundreds of scientific studies, believers:

- Are 25% more likely to live longer.

- Develop less unhealthy lifestyles, such as alcoholism, smoking, snuff use, and unprotected sex.

- They are more likely to wear a seat belt, visit the dentist regularly, and take vitamins.

- Have a more comprehensive social safety net.

- Cope better with stress and psychological problems in challenging situations.

- Exercise stronger willpower and self-discipline.

- They put God's will, family values, and social harmony above others.

- Can prioritize more effectively.

- More often, critically evaluate their actions, words, and deeds.

- More effectively follow instructions.

- They are often looking for long-term benefits rather than a moment's pleasure.

Researchers have also measured people's brain waves when they pray and found that the same areas of the brain that regulate willpower and self-discipline are activated when people pray. If you want to develop your willpower, you can pray to God, and your willpower will develop automatically! And if you're not a believer, you can pray, *"Dear God, help me to know you,"* and you'll get the same benefit. And maybe, as a bonus, you'll find God already waiting for you (God doesn't force anyone to come to Him).

How can self-discipline be developed?

First, we need to change the meaning of *self-discipline* for ourselves. The word discipline typically has a negative connotation. At least for me, the first thing that comes to mind is the discipline I received when I was a child, and things did not go the way others wanted. Self-discipline implies that we should somehow make ourselves suffer when we do something wrong or when we don't do something when we should. We are already disciplined enough by others in life, so why should we discipline ourselves even more? A better definition of self-discipline is Elbert Hubbard's (20th-century American writer) phrase: Self-discipline is the ability to do what you should do *when you should do it, whether you feel like it or not*. So today, self-discipline to me means the same as self-improvement. It is the possibility to grow and develop as a person by shaping my thinking and ways of doing things (especially internally). So, from now on, this book will use the word self-development, not self-discipline! You will see that self-development is a fundamental characteristic of achieving results. Here are five steps to self-development that will help you focus your energy and time on more valuable choices in life:

1. The first step in self-development is to become self-aware in thought and action. We all have buttons that are pushed by our thoughts, the opinions of others, the media, and circumstances. The better we control these buttons, the better we can choose how we act and think in each situation. A person who does not know oneself will quickly find oneself on the wrong track because the world more than quickly takes one by surprise. Reactive living also leads to unwanted responses (for example, saying things to others you shouldn't have).

2. The second step is to be able to control your buttons. This means consciously managing your responses, emotions, and desires, especially under pressure. From my own experience, I can say that this task is very challenging but yields significant results. Choosing whether to eat a chocolate bar, an avocado, and a few nuts in the evening is challenging but very important to complete 500 abdominal muscle movements. Significant actions do not meet big goals but are achieved by a steady stream of small right actions and decisions. Each choice will take you either closer or further away from your goals. More

than 70% of your choices must take you closer rather than further away. *See, these are not unreasonable demands. Bad choices from time to time are part of human life and, therefore, should also be factored into your plans and allowed to slip up without losing sight of the grand prize.*

3. The third principle that supports healthy self-development is the ability to say NO. And that is sometimes difficult but important. When your brain is screaming at you to lie on the couch and watch TV when you should be writing a book, you must be able to say a firm NO to yourself. Here's a simple psychological trick for such a case: tell yourself you will watch TV tomorrow, but today you shall write. That way, you do not have to force yourself but have chosen to do it tomorrow. Of course, you will make this choice again tomorrow, but don't tell yourself that now. Such a brain hack will get you through those moments when you don't have the resources to say NO.

4. The fourth important thing is to learn to delay getting pleasure and to redefine what gives you pleasure. This means putting aside momentary cravings for greater satisfaction in the longer term. For example, consider a situation where you have $ 2,000 cash to buy a car. Let's imagine you could save $500 a month. You can save for six more months and buy a better car for $5,000 or buy a $2,000 car today. If you buy a cheaper, worse-conditioned vehicle today, you may see how much money will be wasted on repairing and towing it. But if you find alternative ways to get around for six months, you'll end up with a car that lasts better and saves you money in the future with lower unexpected maintenance costs. Sure, it's easy to say in hindsight that it's worth saving up and buying a better one, but it takes skill now; hindsight no longer fixes the current situation (although it certainly helps you learn for future problems). This is why I have never had a single consumer credit or outstanding credit card payment. It is better to save

and buy what I need without debt than to pay it off with 40% interest.

5. The fifth factor in self-development is to accept that moving forward, acquiring skills, achieving challenging things, and maximizing your life potential requires being in what is known as an area of discomfort (I prefer to call it a growth area). A simple rule of thumb is that if you are too comfortable, you are not developing and not using all the resources you could have. Sure, it's nice, but it's not necessarily developing. If there is one reason that prevents people from exceeding themselves and their goals, it is this: *the desire to be comfortable too easily overpowers the desire to develop.* But you and I know better; we deliberately get into growth territory because we know it will take us forward in the long run. I remember the first time I did planking: even a 30-second plank was painful; my whole body was shaking, and every brain cell in my head was screaming to *STOP.* But the longer I stayed in that growth zone, the more my muscles gave in, and nowadays, I go for five minutes as a regular warm-up. And yes, my muscles are still shaking, and my brain is screaming for mercy, but the plank stays on and lasts longer over time.

Self-development is about changing your perspective from the nice things you do to the results you want to get. I had virtually no interest in exercise for the first 40 years of my life. One excuse for this was that I was always picked last for the sports at school and was usually asked to stay out of the way while other, more skilled players played. But at one point in my mid-30s, I saw a TV series about the American Navy Seals, particularly their extreme week-long endurance test called *Hell Week*[*]. Although I didn't see myself as a musclehead any more than a realistic candidate for such a week, I was fascinated by the idea of developing myself on such a megalomaniacal scale. I dug up all the information I

---

[*] https://www.youtube.com/watch?v=KCL6TikUoWQ

could find about them: movies, books, and biographies, too. At the same time, I also learned that there was a similar force in England called the SAS. Because I lived in England, I started following Ant Middleton, Ollie Ollerton, and other SAS guys training regular people on special forces fitness goals. That started my fitness and running enthusiasm, from 200m to half marathons (with 40 pounds weight in a rucksack) to gym programs, long cold baths, and other things that some people think are crazy. The pain of training is immense, but the thought of passing that fitness test is so exciting that I can't help but keep going! What would be something as exciting for you?

When was the last time you invested in your development and learning?

Many do not train at all after leaving university or vocational school. The American Education Association[*] has researched how much the top 20% of successful companies invest in staff learning, around 3%. This same rule of thumb is a good starting point: invest at least 3% of your income in your education to increase your value in the market. According to statistics, 87% of Finns earn less than $ 50,000 a year, so they should spend up to $ 1,500 a year on personal development. When was the last time you did this? That money can't get you very far, especially on expensive courses, so knowing where you want to go and what will get you there is even more critical. Otherwise, money is easily wasted on wrong training. Of course, with the same money, you can buy many books and online courses which provide a lot of good information. And don't forget the beneficial accessible sources of information such as YouTube, Wikipedia, and others. Self-development daily is essential to increase your skills. Here are some easy ways to keep learning new things without exhausting yourself:

- ♦ Read, listen, and watch daily non-fiction materials related to your goals. The TV is very unlikely to do anything to help your

---

[*] American Society of Training and Development

development, so leave it out and read something useful instead. Our family hasn't watched aerial channels for over a decade, and no one has complained (except for overnight guests who wonder why the TV doesn't work).

- Watch and listen to audiobooks and online videos while doing other, less productive things. For example, commuting is an excellent opportunity to learn through audiobooks. For example, my fifth book, *Marry Your Customer*, was primarily written on commuter trains in London, UK. Of course, just listening and watching doesn't do it - you also need to think about what the information means, whether it's helpful to you, and, if so, how you will put it into practice.

- Attend courses, events, and networking opportunities to gain knowledge and experience relevant to your goals. These can take place face-to-face or online. Never stop learning.

One critical area to develop in life is relationship management. In this world, it is virtually impossible to succeed without other people. Whenever more than two people are around, the potential for conflict is high, at least at some point in the relationship. But successful people have neither the time nor the energy for long-term feuds and grudges. It is not fruitful for anyone (although sometimes it seems that some people have made holding grudges their primary purpose in life, reflecting their ability to add value to others). However, it is impossible to avoid difficult situations with others, so how can we improve ourselves to resolve things as quickly and satisfactorily as possible for all parties involved? Here are some ideas that have been proven to work:

- First, don't try to converse if one of the parties is in intense emotion, such as anger or rage. When you are in this state, your brain is driven by primitive functions, and having a rational conversation is impossible. So, wait for a better situation or try to change the person's mind to a more favorable one. This also works for you if you are in turmoil in any situation. Find peace as quickly as possible to move on in a better frame of mind. In an intense emotional state, conversation is not helpful.

- Let others express their opinions and feelings; your turn will come. Please don't interrupt; no matter how much they may be talking, it will help defuse the situation (also, don't take what they say personally in this state of mind).

- Do your best to actively listen to the other person and guide the conversation and the situation with questions, not comments. Read their body language to see which way the problem is going.

- If you habitually finish other people's sentences, eliminate this bad habit altogether. This habit is particularly harmful in conflict situations, but it's of no use at other times.

- Don't assume anything, but survive. People's brains work in very different ways, so what you think or interpret may not be the same as what someone else does. So it's better to find out than to explain.

- If your opinions differ, find things you agree on and build on them to develop solutions further. Spend less energy looking for differences than for similarities.

- This may seem strange, but when the other person is done explaining, ask them if they want to add anything before jumping in with your thoughts. This allows them to recap the main points if they want to, and it also makes them think that you're genuinely interested in resolving the situation.

- If you don't understand or agree with something, ask more specific questions. Most of the time, Nokia's old *"not invented here"* mindset is vital in people, so you are better off getting them to change their minds through questions than through direct words. Although you are probably right, and the facts may be on your side, people are sometimes blind until they invent what you have just tried to explain.

- Once you have reached this stage, you can factually present your views, referring to the facts and what the other person has said. You are like a lawyer* who builds a conversation that guides others in your desired direction.

Here are some good phrases to use in conflict situations:

I don't quite understand everything you mean yet, could you tell me more...?

Please help me understand/know more about this issue that worries/frightens you.

Perhaps I have been a bit inflexible on this; what are your recommendations for improving the situation?

Could we think together about the best options to resolve this situation for both of us?

I would like to know what you think about this.

Can I share with you how I see this situation from my side?

It seems you do not have all the relevant information, so I want to tell you what I know about this issue.

As you probably noticed, the aim is not to overwhelm the other person with your ideas but to steer the conversation as quickly and efficiently as possible to a situation where a solution can be agreed upon and a way forward can be found. And this is rarely achieved by hammering in our ideas. It is more like fishing, where the fish must be tired and guided into the net until it can be caught without a fight. Perhaps the biblical idea of *doing unto others as you would have them do unto you* (*Matthew 7:12*) works here. None of us wants to be humiliated or subjugated (and perhaps that's why so many, in their anger, overreact to establish their opinions as superior).

---

* You should read Gerry Spencer's book "*How to argue and win every time*".

In this chapter, we have discussed self-development from the perspective of achieving challenging goals. Self-discipline, willpower, self-development, and social skills will help you succeed, whatever your goals are. Many skills require concentration and can be challenging but rewarding, so in the next chapter, we will continue with the theme of moving forward and perseverance.

The reason for coping

A Jewish survivor of Auschwitz, Viktor E. Frankl, says that apart from God's protection, the main reason he survived, unlike millions of others, was that he wanted to live more. He wanted to finish his psychological framework called logotherapy before he died. He scribbled his book about it on scraps of paper in the concentration camp cells (whenever he could from his forced labor work). He tells of a study in which 89% of people said having a reason to live was essential. In another study, thousands of people were asked what was crucial, and 78% said the most important thing was to find a purpose for their lives (only 16% said the most important thing was to make a lot of money). This truth was starkly illustrated in the concentration camps: there was a rumor among the prisoners that they would be released on the first Christmas. This kept the spirits of those who had heard and believed this rumor until Christmas. But then Christmas came and went, but no freedom was granted. Most of those who had been very hopeful of their deliverance died in the next few days and weeks after Christmas, having lost both their hope and their reason to live. According to Viktor, the best way to keep going is to find a purpose for oneself that gives one the strength to take steps forward when one's feet no longer carry one. Very soon after arriving at the camp, Viktor learned that the length of his life was directly proportional to his motivation. Most gave up and soon died, either at the hands of the Germans or by their own hands. Viktor faced the same physical challenges as the others (such as building roads for the Germans in winter barefoot, constant torture, lack of food, and disease and parasites). But he thought very differently and knew that having a strong enough reason to live would help him overcome his difficulties. After his release from the camp, he moved to the US and developed logotherapy, which focuses on helping people find their purpose. Of course, he was blessed too, as no positive thinking, or any other force than God, would have saved him from a murderous nazi if it was to be so.

The basis for perseverance, whether in life or in doing anything challenging, is a sufficiently motivating reason to keep going (believers hope that God will take care of their own). And that reason cannot be bought or taken from others but must be found deep within oneself. Of course, others can help you find your reasons through coaching, but everyone must find their own reasons for living and reaching challenging goals. The search for purpose in life is not necessarily a peaceful process but sometimes a painful one, as Viktor experienced. Nietzsche has said it well: *He who has a reason* to *live can live any life.* That is why humans repeatedly evaluate our reasons for living and doing things and how they affect our current well-being (like whether maintaining your health is important enough for you to go out for a jog even when it is pouring rain). If you go to training courses for successful motivational speakers, they very often have a lecture where you write down a life mission. They do this because they won't get very far in their endeavors if people don't have an apparent, sufficiently motivating reason to live or do things. Some unscrupulous lecturers take this exploitation of psychological need to the point of making participants write down on paper why they should buy whatever the lecturer is selling and how they would suffer if they didn't buy. And as a result, people literally rush to sign the long purchase contracts with no cancellation options. After all, they just wrote down why they have good reasons to do so!

Humans have an inbuilt need to find meaning in our lives, so much so that it forms the basis of our mental health. Since meaning in life is the most essential thing for almost everyone, it is no surprise that an imbalance in this can cause a wide range of mental health problems. A healthy mind is a balance between what a person has already achieved and what they could still achieve, and what each person is today and what they could still become. Too often, we try to eliminate these conflicting ideas from our minds and either settle for too little or strive for the impossible. What is your situation right now? Answer these questions to find out:

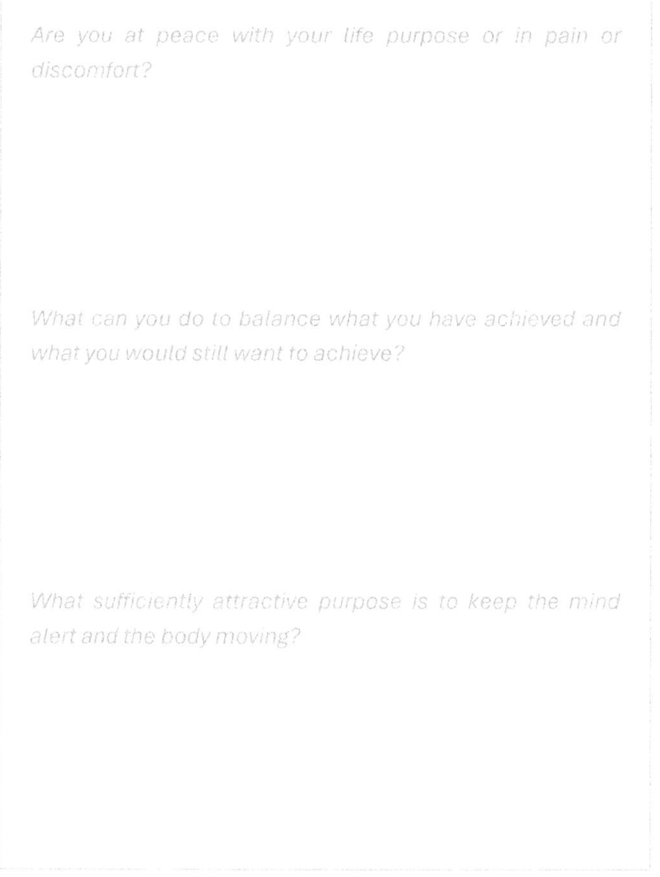

If you don't have good enough answers to these questions, your first task is to find them. Depending on the research, 25-60% of people live in a constant state of lack of purpose in life. This leads to different symptoms depending on the person. Some experience it as boredom. Others try to fill the hole with drugs, sex, watching TV, and many other vain or destructive activities. Others passivate and do little or nothing. Some get depressed and suffer emotionally or end their lives prematurely. These are the consequences, not the root cause that needs fixing. Many people also tend to forget how much worse things could be (famine, war, and chronic poverty in many countries). The lack of purpose in life has even gone so far for some that there is a psychological condition called *Sunday neurosis*. It refers to the leisure-induced depression that strikes people who lack a sense of purpose in life when they don't have to work. In London, there is a phenomenon called the *Monday train*, which refers to the fact that people are most likely to jump on a train track on Monday mornings. Having lived in London for almost ten years, I can confirm that this is a real problem at certain times of the year when trains cannot run on schedule on Mondays because of suicides. This makes me very sad because we all have a purpose and a place in this world; we have not all tried to find it. *"For I know the plans I have for you, declares the Lord, plans for welfare and not for evil, to give you a future and a hope"* (Jeremiah 29:11).

Are you deadwood?

Nick Vujicic is a philanthropist and motivational speaker. He is one of the most inspiring people I have met (the good thing about living in London is that many people come to give lectures there, and it's easy to meet them). Nick is a Serbian-Australian man who was born with *tetra-amelia syndrome*. He has virtually no arms and no legs. You can imagine what kind of start to life you get in this world without limbs. He was so desperate about his situation that he tried to kill himself. Thank God Nick began to talk about his situation in his prayer group and found meaning in his life through that. Today, he runs an international anti-bullying charity and leads a Christian organization, *Life Without Limbs*, which supports people with disabilities worldwide. One of Nick's passions is giving highly motivational talks to young school people, not just crying but also agreeing on concrete actions to reduce bullying. Many young people give their lives to Jesus, inspired by Nick and moved by the Holy Spirit. I can only imagine what life would have been like at my secondary school if someone like this had visited us. Regardless, we should learn from everything we experience and use it as a resource and lesson to further develop our purpose in life. *What about you? Do you submit to being someone's victim, or do you take your life into your own hands?*

Perhaps we need to turn our approach to this question the other way around. Instead of looking everywhere for a purpose in life, we need to decide it. Thus, maybe the question, *"What is my purpose in life?"* is sometimes fruitless and only causes anxiety. The question should not be asked of the world, people, or things but of ourselves and our God. Life asks this question of us, not the other way around! We are responsible for everything in our lives, not just some aspects*. Circumstances, opinions, news, events, experts, or others should not determine your purpose. If you let others determine your purpose, you become a victim, a passenger in your life. Your life is unique, one of a kind. No one or nothing can replace you in this world. *You are perfectly created as you already are. What are you going to do with it?* That is up to you and your choices.

Of course, such choices should not happen in a vacuum, without interaction with the Holy Spirit, other people, and the world. We have many examples of what happens when a person chooses a vacuum. School shooters, criminals, child abusers, and even the former US President, Donald Trump, have answered the question of their purpose of existence from very selfish perspectives. And while they have chosen for themselves, this choice still has a direct impact on the lives of others. It is essential to realize that whatever we choose will always affect others. After all, none of us are acting purely for ourselves but also for others. Perhaps this explains people's inner need to fulfill and exceed themselves in worthy pursuits that bring good to others (such as charity).

---

* Which makes what Jesus did even more miraculous because he did not commit our sins, but only atoned for them.

Every moment of life is a choice

We have countless opportunities at every moment. These opportunities pass us by, wait for us, or realize themselves. The opportunities that do come to fruition are the ones that develop and move us forward. They become part of us and our history, and the other opportunities that existed at that moment either pass us by or continue to wait. **We are responsible for all the choices we make.** This makes us active agents rather than passive observers or victims of circumstances. Even those who have chosen to give the power of decision over their own lives to others have made this decision at some point.

Stephen R. Covey's book *The 7 Habits of Highly Effective People: Powerful Lessons in Personal Change"* has excellent lessons that have helped millions worldwide. The book introduces a tool called *the Circle of Influence,* which is an excellent tool to help you focus on the right things. It is a way of thinking that focuses on finding solutions rather than worrying about problems. The Circle of Influence has two circles. The inner circle contains the things we can influence, and the outer circle contains the things beyond our control. It is easy for people to fall into the trap of thinking and focusing only on the things outside the circle, i.e., those that are beyond their control (e.g., wars, famine, nuclear bombs, bad news, what our neighbors do, what idiotic things Trump says, etc.). This way of thinking leads to wasting energy on the wrong things and causes feelings of unhappiness and hopelessness. And when a person spends their energy on these things in the outer circle, they are also reducing the focus on the things in their own circle of influence, because we all have a limited amount of time and energy available. In simple terms, a person's life focused on the outer circle is filled with thoughts that make them anxious and unhappy. Instead, concentrating on the inner circle is an effective way to make the best use of one's energy and to increase happiness.

The coronavirus (which likely came from a lab in Wuhan, China) grounded most people worldwide for almost two years. It was an extremely stressful time for many, leading to job termination, anxiety, and many other issues. Even in such extreme situations, an empowered mindset gives individuals the strength to cope with everyday life. It increases their sense of control over their lives through a sense of achievement. Thus, it is better to redirect focus to solutions rather than dwelling on problems. Such shaping of one's thinking helps in a challenging situation where the attention may divert easily to the outer edge of the Circle of Influence. So, how could you use this powerful tool to increase your resilience? Here's an exercise for you:

1.   Use several pieces of paper and a pen during this exercise.

2.   Take one piece of paper and draw what you think a good day looks like. Don't write anything, draw. And it doesn't matter if it seems like the output of a preschool art exhibition.

3.   Now, take another piece of paper and repeat the same exercise, but draw what a lousy day would look like for you. Again, don't write anything; draw to the limits of your ability.

4.   Take another piece of paper (not a tree-friendly exercise, sorry) and draw a big circle on it (as big as the paper will fit). This circle is your Circle of Concern. It contains all the things that worry, depress, or upset you.

5.   Now draw a slightly smaller circle (not too small) inside this big circle. If you're as talented a drawer as I am, you should now have two circles on paper that look like a fried egg. I've put these two circles below this exercise so you can use them. This smaller circle is your circle of influence. You can do something about the things inside it.

6.   Look back at your good day paper and pick the three most important things that could impact your day.

7.   Then look at your lousy day paper and pick the three most important things that would improve your day if they were changed for the better.

8. Put these six things inside the Circles of Influence you drew earlier. Which ones go inside the Circle of Influence (smaller), inside the Circle of Concern (larger), and which are entirely outside?

9. See where these things ended up. If they are within your Circle of Influence, they are things you can focus on, and they will improve your day. Everything else outside the smaller circle is outside your influence, so you can stop wasting more of your time on them. You can't do anything about it anyway.

10. Think about the purpose of this exercise and how you can start using this as an easy exercise to do in your head when you notice things starting to worry you. For me, this has boiled down to a simple question: is there anything I can do about the thing I'm worrying about right now? If the answer is no, I don't

think about it anymore. If yes, I use the other tools described in this book to determine its importance and next steps.

Most of our lives happen inside our heads as perceptions and interpretations of what's happening around us. So, tools like the one above can very quickly increase our resilience, happiness, and effectiveness because we make the best use of our time. Here are some more examples of everyday things that can be inside your Circle of Influence:

- ♦ A positive attitude, whatever the situation

- ♦ My reactions to things

- ♦ What I say to others

- ♦ Limiting consumption

- ♦ Doing nice things

- ♦ Your kindness and helpfulness towards others

- ♦ Quantity and quality of physical activity

- ♦ Optimizing the quantity and quality of your sleep

- ♦ Optimizing your productivity and efficiency

- ♦ How I spend my time and with whom

- ♦ Setting and achieving your own goals

- ♦ Content I consume (books, programs, music, etc.)

- ♦ My knowledge and skills

- ♦ All the things I want to keep doing

Here are some examples of things that could be in the Circle of Concern:

- ♦ Managing what others do and say

- Other people's motivations and behavior

- Predicting the future

- Most news content and their negative style

- Unexpected problems

- Other people's reactions to things

- Famine, war, natural disasters, death

- Gossip, talking behind your back, opinions

- World and national economy, recession

- When will the films be released and how good are they?

- How others spend their time and with whom

- Skills and qualifications of others

Sometimes, all it takes to keep going is to take the first step toward what you need to do, and the rest of the steps will take themselves almost automatically from there. Don't just go where things are easiest; it's simply not rewarding in the long run. Also, don't be misled by emotions; development happens in the growth area, not outside it. Your life will be gratifying because you will know what to do to get there. I learned this, for example, in weightlifting at the gym. Even though I went there several times a week, I didn't see more muscle coming up. One day, I decided to pull double weights on the bar, put an emergency number on the phone, and see what happened. Sure, there were significantly fewer repetitions and more pain, but the weights moved. I did the same thing again the following few times and found quickly that this double weight became a new base for me. I'm not saying that the weights in any way started to feel lighter, but I found that I could take more of the pain they caused and, therefore, get results faster. And yes, the muscles started to develop, too!

Every day and every night that your heart beats

Inside you, there is a battle between what is correct and valuable and what is easy and fun but doesn't move you forward. Recognize this fact, focus on your reasons to do what needs to be done, and take that first step, then the second. You will only turn your inner purring cat into a roaring, brave lion that gets things done. And when the going gets tough, remember that you knew it would happen. You can say, *well, I knew this would be a challenge, so I'll solve it immediately.* You shouldn't be surprised when it happens but should be ready to laugh in the face of adversity. There is an old saying in England from the Second World War: *keep calm and carry on,* which is still true today. Let's keep looking forward and facing difficulties because that's where we grow up. There is no room for self-pity as we are not victims. Each of us is an adult, responsible for our own lives and, above all, for our choices about how we deal with things and circumstances. We also do not point the finger at anyone; we forgive, and we do what we can to ensure that no one or nothing can stop us from achieving our goals. This is how winners think! They think about what they can do to resolve the situation and take the first steps towards solutions as soon as possible.

Norman Vincent Peale, an American minister in the 1960s[*], said that when God wants to give you a gift, he wraps it in a challenge. And the bigger the gift, the bigger the challenges it comes with. We should see challenges as a way to grow and become stronger. The lessons learned from these challenges will help us endure and overcome future challenges. Once you have decided that nothing can stop you, you become invincible, and the only one who can stop you is you and God.

Have you heard about Mike Hughes, who believed in a flat earth[†]? Even though he had flown in an airplane and seen a curved horizon, he believed the earth was flat. He thought the best way to prove the Earth was flat was to build his steam-powered rocket and fly it high enough

---

[*] https://en.wikipedia.org/wiki/Norman_Vincent_Peale
[†] https://metro.co.uk/2020/02/23/man-dies-homemade-rocket-crashes-mission-prove-earth-flat-12286807/

to see the flatness of the Earth and take a picture of it (apparently, he missed all the other images taken from space?). However, the rocket's parachute opened too early; the rocket only flew about 500 yards, and the view of the flatness of the earth was missed. Mike landed on a desert ridge and flattened himself. While his perseverance and guts were admirable, it might have been worth testing the first flight, even if it was with a neighbor's dog rather than his own life. Well, at least he won the Darwin Award[*].

Go back to your earlier exercise about your life purpose and add details. Some of the questions below are difficult, and it's okay to think about the answers. It's worth writing them down in the box below, or even in your journal, so that you can come back to them and develop your answers as your life progresses (which it will, whether or not you develop your purpose).

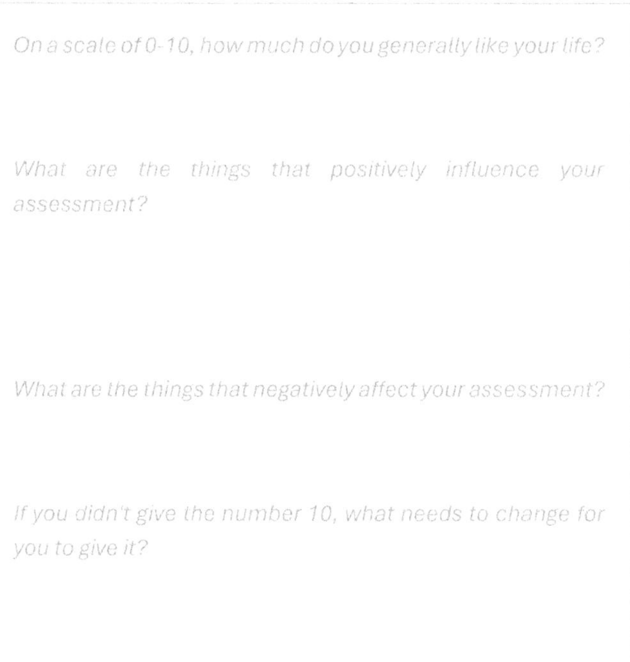

---

[*] https://darwinawards.com/rules/

Do you like what you do for a living these days? What would you have to change in your job to make you like it more?

Do you like your hobbies? What would you have to change in your hobbies to make you like them even more?

What would you like to achieve in your life? And why these things? How would you feel if you achieved these things?

What would be the things you would keep going towards despite the difficulties?

What do you think you are good at?

What do others praise you for?

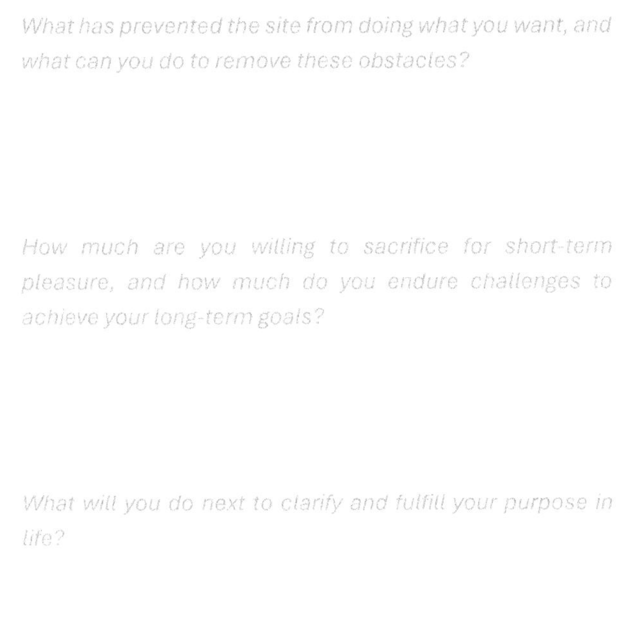

In this chapter, we have gone through some of the perhaps somewhat tricky coping-related issues. In today's world, where the *#efficiencyeconomy* is trying to squeeze every ounce of juice out of us, the importance of purpose in our lives and goals is even more critical than ever. It helps us focus our energy on the right things and do things that grow and develop us rather than consuming us.

Recognize the facts

What would you say if I argued that Donald Trump (the crazy ex-American president), Mother Teresa (the empathetic international philanthropist), and the Pope (the Catholic religious leader) are all driven by similar motivations? Probably, some phrase along the lines of *don't be ridiculous* comes readily to mind. What could they have in common, then?

Like all of ours, their actions are driven by the need to gain pleasure and satisfaction and ***avoid pain and suffering***. So, where do these people differ? In the meaning they give to the things that provide them with pleasure or distress. They have gone to very different extremes in their choices. Donald Trump gets pleasure from exalting himself and his fortune. He takes no pleasure in consideration of others or charity. For Mother Teresa, these had the opposite effect: for her, wealth was not substantial; it was helping others that gave her pleasure. Conversely, the Pope gets pleasure from promoting the Catholic religion and values, which he believes help others. So, to generalize a little, all these people are acting with the same base motives but responding to the same need in very different ways. They have chosen different meanings for things in their lives. Of course, their background and where they have grown up and lived have influenced their choices, but ultimately, it has been their own choice. And so, it is with you, too. The things you like or dislike have likely come to you from your environment and experiences. But you also have the power and authority to choose meanings differently (or keep the current ones). You can decide whether money is the most essential thing to you or just a tool. You can choose how much you enjoy (or hate) helping others. And as you probably already deduced from the examples above, your choices determine the kind of person you become and the outcomes you achieve in life. This also allows us to use this technique to strengthen the valuable things in our lives and eliminate the unhelpful ones. We can associate unpleasantness with stuff we no longer want; thus, our minds begin to avoid them rather than want them. Similarly, we can associate pleasure with things we didn't like before and thus make our minds wish for them more.

Have you ever thought about where your current desires for pleasure come from? Firstly, most of us have not necessarily chosen them consciously or purposefully. Secondly, many of our beliefs are based on past experiences, and thirdly, we quickly forget that these beliefs are only interpretations of our experiences, not necessarily their actual manifestations. For example, when we have been to the hairdresser and our friend (or spouse) does not immediately notice or compliment it, we may interpret that they are not interested in us (which may or may not be true). One psychological study interviewed people who had been in the same bus accident just over ten years ago. The accident was so tragic that some of the passengers died. Now, a decade later, some of the surviving passengers were so traumatized by the experience that they had psychological and substance abuse problems that had started after the event. Some had gone on with their lives as before. And a few had redesigned their lives and produced significantly more value for themselves and others than before the accident. They were all in the same accident and experienced the same thing. But how they interpreted the experience and what meaning they gave to it was very different. For some, it was an empowering experience, and for others, a crippling one. They had a choice about which camp they belonged to, and their lives fully reflected that choice. I saw such a choice in very concrete terms when a family friend of ours, just over 30 years old, was diagnosed with pancreatic cancer and died about three months after diagnosis. He could have moaned about his fate and died in hospital in misery. But he chose Christian missionary work instead, broadcasting what he called a "sickbed sermon" from his laptop in the hospital. He felt he gave his all in the last weeks of his life, and through him, hundreds of young adults found their way to salvation with Jesus. And how much their changed lives will help others, so our friends' memories live on in a very tangible way through hundreds of others.

What kind of beliefs do you have? Let's start with your most common beliefs. Complete the sentences below:

Life for me is...

I am...

People are...

Be honest with yourself. Do the things you wrote above include your most common beliefs? Now look at them again and consider which of these beliefs are beneficial and bring you pleasure and which are harmful or cause you or others distress.

The beliefs that give me pleasure/benefit:

The beliefs that cause me distress/harm:

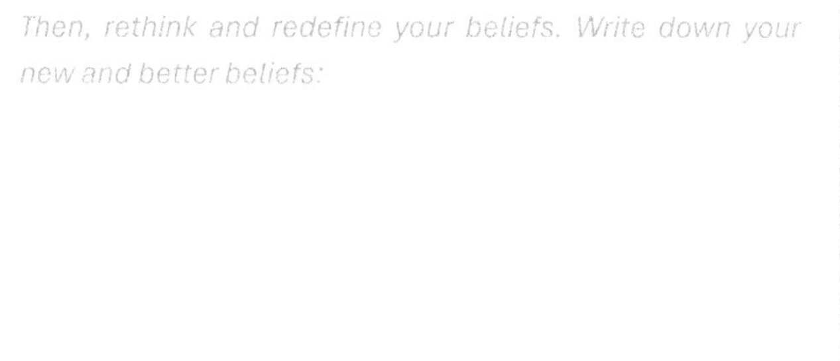

Congratulations, you have now taken a concrete step (perhaps for the first time in your life) towards awareness of your beliefs and their impact on your life. Anthony Robbins recommends you also consider the following three beliefs that can make life more positive:

1. ***Things must change and evolve, and standing still is not an option.*** It would be best if you were convinced that you want to improve things. Not tomorrow or someday, but today.

2. ***The one who needs to change their beliefs is you.*** Not your friends, parents, spouse, children, or anyone else. You need to see yourself as the source and agent of change.

3. ***You can change things.*** It would be best if you believed in the power within you that you can use and grow to change things yourself.

With these three beliefs firmly embedded, you can create sustainable, iterative development in your life and the lives of others. Of course, it is possible to make a short-term, temporary change without them, but we are not interested in that because the benefits are too small. You are the master of your own life! And perhaps you are wondering why you go through all that trouble. Because you know that these are the ways to get results that last. Being a victim is useless. Both you and others around you will have a better life with you when you live it to the fullest.

How do you spend your time?

We are rarely aware of how we spend our time (often, time is spent on very different things than we think it is). Managing our time is very important as we have a very finite amount of time available. As mentioned, *time is the world's greatest equalizer; no one can add or subtract hours in a day, whether a king, a priest, a worker, or a billionaire.* Therefore, time management is a vital skill to ensure success. I recommend that you start keeping an accurate diary of what you do daily to get an idea of where your time goes. I use an electronic calendar for this purpose to update what's coming up (time management plans) and where that time went (diary). You can use the space below for a week to record where your time goes:

I spent my time on MONDAY on these things:

I spent my time on these things on TUESDAY:

I spent my WEDNESDAY on these things:

I spent my time on THURSDAY on these things:

Now you know where your time is going. You can move on to the next step and plan how to spend your time on weekdays and weekends. For example, you could put more emphasis on work and learning on weekdays and more on exercise, family, and recovery on weekends. Use the formula below to plan your time use:

- There are 24 hours each day, seven days a week, so you have 168 hours each week.

- Assuming you sleep the recommended 8 hours a night, that's 56 hours.

- Let's assume you work 8 hours daily, five days a week. So that's 40 hours.

- You also set aside 4 hours daily to get to work and prepare for it (such as hygiene, dressing, and cooking). This takes up 28 hours of your week.

♦ After these activities, 44 hours a week, or about 6 hours a day, are available for other things. Now, the question is, how do you plan to use it? Here's an example of how to divide your time on workdays:

- Half an hour for brisk exercise
- Children and family 2 hours
- 1 hour for learning and self-development
- Advancing your goals 1 hour
- Relaxing and meditating for 1 hour
- Flexibility time: half an hour

♦ On your days off, you have 8 hours more to spend because you don't have to go to work. How do you use this time in addition to the above? Maybe you can add time for family, learning, and advancing your goals. It will also leave time for socializing, relaxing, and recuperating (in a sauna).

If you are a student, you will naturally spend your time studying instead of working. And if you're a pensioner, you can decide whether to spend your weekdays differently from your weekends or to make a similar time plan for all days. Make your time management plan now:

How I spend my time on weekdays:

How I use my time on my days off:

What did the time management plan make you think? Are you surprised by the results when you compare it with the time diary you made earlier? This exercise is a good reminder that there is no time to waste.

According to research, the hours spent watching TV have doubled since the 1990s to more than three hours a day. This is even though social media, among other things, is taking up an increasing slice of people's time. Is it any wonder that there is no time left for more important things when so much time is wasted daily?

Another significant time waster is *alcohol*. There is sufficient scientific evidence that alcohol in quantities greater than one beer or glass of wine daily is bad for you. On the upside, there is also research evidence that one beer or glass of red wine a day can add up to 10 years to your life. However, I am sad to say that the average alcohol consumption, for example, in Finland, is around 2 gallons of 100% alcohol per year per adult. Drinking alcohol wastes time twice, first when you drink and then when you have a hangover. Calculate how many hours or days you have wasted in the last six months drinking and hangover. So why do so many people gravitate toward drinking? According to a study by Annemari von Forstmeyer, up to 90% of alcoholics have felt their lives were meaningless. Thus, it is easy to fill the feeling of emptiness with booze instead of looking for things that are meaningful and more sustainable than chemical stimulants.

A third time-saving factor is reducing *the information overload*. You don't need to know everything that's going on in the world all the time. I stopped actively following the news almost ten years ago and still know what's happening in the world adequately. If an issue is important enough, others will discuss it, and you can investigate it in more detail. I've been in a few social situations where people talk about yesterday's football match or some other event (for example, once someone asked me what I thought of Greta Thunberg), and I didn't even know what they were talking about. However, once I have quickly searched online to find out what it's about, I've often found that I haven't missed anything important. I know, without following the doomsday news every day, that the climate is warming, the earth is not flat, and there is a lot of bad stuff happening all over the world every day (for some reason, the news doesn't care to report any of the good things happening). So, it's safe for you to limit your news and social media intake and spend less time on them. In addition, cancel all your newsletter subscriptions (unless they add value to your Top 5 goals). They only clog up your email account and take up time. Watch out for other emails, too, as they are too easy to send. It doesn't take more than a couple of minutes to send someone a message asking to do something, but the task can take the recipient months without even being important. Moreover, email is written text, which is extremely easy to misunderstand. Thus, it is recommended that going forward you use email very carefully and thoughtfully asking questions such as:

- Do I need to send this message at all?

- How else can I communicate this?

- What is essential in this message?

- How will the recipient interpret my message?

If only we could stop for even 10 seconds and think about the message before hitting that send button, many things would go better.

The next time-saving factor can anger people, but it is essential. It would be best if you avoided *people who waste your time*. We are all surrounded by those who take energy rather than give it. They talk too much and say too little. They always have needs that others should meet. They ask for advice but do not accept it. Such people are energy wasters and should be avoided as much as possible. I am asked for advice on many things, and I have decided to give advice the first time and then ask what the person will do. I then ask what they have achieved since the previous advice if they ask for advice again. And if no progress has been made, I won't spend more time advising them. But if progress has been made, I will give more advice. Many in this world progress things, and even more those who do nothing. Alas, spending time with those who make things happen and multiply what they receive is better. Another group of people to avoid are the perpetual complainers. They are the ones for whom the weather is never good enough; life always kicks them in the head, and generally speaking, something is always wrong. There are indeed many things in their lives, and ours, that could be better, but successful people know that complaining achieves nothing and is a waste of time and energy. It only adds negative energy and empowers mental victimization. You may be surprised by this, but we should also avoid over-positive people who are not in touch with reality. The kind of person who always finds the silver lining in everything without acknowledging the actual state of things cannot help you. It doesn't do much good if you lose your leg in a motorcycle accident and the person consoles you that at least you still have to keep your arm. Instead, a person who offers help (according to what you need) would be much more valuable.

What does luck have to do with anything?

How well do you know your capacity for development? Have you ever thought about it? Most of us haven't. Yet it is vital to change your attitude and outlook to be more growing and to focus on promoting those areas where you have the most room for improvement. Let's do a simple test to help you know yourself better in a developmental capacity. Follow the instructions in the test to get the most out of it. Answer the statements below on a scale of 0 to 10, with zero being left-hand and ten being right-hand. Give yourself a number that describes your situation and your mindset today. So now pick up a pen and circle the numbers on each line:

Mapping the current situation

I plan to start tomorrow.
0 1 2 3 4 5 6 7 8 9 10
I will start today.

I expect my development to come by itself.
0 1 2 3 4 5 6 7 8 9 10
I improve myself every day.

I learn from mistakes.
0 1 2 3 4 5 6 7 8 9 10
I learn already before I make mistakes

I'm counting on good luck
0 1 2 3 4 5 6 7 8 9 10
I rely on hard work.

I give up easily/early.
0 1 2 3 4 5 6 7 8 9 10
I will persist and continue for a long time

I have bad habits
0 1 2 3 4 5 6 7 8 9 10
I reinforce my good habits.

I talk more than I do
0 1 2 3 4 5 6 7 8 9 10
I do more than I talk.

I play it safe.
0 1 2 3 4 5 6 7 8 9 10
I take controlled risks.

I often feel like a victim.
        0 1 2 3 4 5 6 7 8 9 10
                I learn from all experiences.

I develop my skills.
        0 1 2 3 4 5 6 7 8 9 10
                I develop my character.

I have been to school enough.
        0 1 2 3 4 5 6 7 8 9 10
                I am constantly learning new things.

Now add up the scores you gave for each of the 11 rows (for example, 3 + 7 + 2 + 8 + 9 + 1 + 0 +4 + 10 + 12 + 2 = 58) and write down the total here: _____________

Next, divide this sum by 11 and round to the nearest whole number (for example, 58 / 11 = 5). Write the number down below.

My development capacity figure is: _____________

Here's your current development capacity figure. Repeat the exercise and circle where you want to be on each line. Remember that the higher the goal, the more you have to work for it.

Target state

I plan to start tomorrow.
        0 1 2 3 4 5 6 7 8 9 10
                I will start today.

I expect my development to come by itself.
        0 1 2 3 4 5 6 7 8 9 10
                I improve myself every day.

I learn from mistakes.

0 1 2 3 4 5 6 7 8 9 10

I learn already before I make mistakes

I'm counting on good luck

0 1 2 3 4 5 6 7 8 9 10

I rely on hard work.

I give up easily/early.

0 1 2 3 4 5 6 7 8 9 10

I will last and continue for a long time

I have bad habits

0 1 2 3 4 5 6 7 8 9 10

I reinforce my good habits.

I talk more than I do

0 1 2 3 4 5 6 7 8 9 10

I do more than I talk.

I play it safe.

0 1 2 3 4 5 6 7 8 9 10

I take controlled risks.

I often feel like a victim.

0 1 2 3 4 5 6 7 8 9 10

I learn from all experiences.

I develop my skills.

0 1 2 3 4 5 6 7 8 9 10

I develop my character.

I have been to school enough.

0 1 2 3 4 5 6 7 8 9 10

I am constantly learning new things.

Now add up the scores you gave for each of the 11 rows (for example, 3 + 7 + 2 + 8 + 9 + 1 + 0 +4 + 10 + 12 + 2 = 58) and write down the total here:

Next, divide this sum by 11 and round to the nearest whole number (for example, 58 / 11 = 5). Write the number down below.

My target development capacity figure is:

Now you can compare these two different figures and think about the answers to the following questions:

What did you learn from this exercise?

In which areas of development are you already strong?

Where do you have the most room for improvement?

How will you start to develop these areas?

How will this information help you optimize your ability to
achieve the goals you want in life?

Now that you have examined yourself from a development perspective,
you can also look around you. While the overall theme of this book is
that we are not victims and, therefore, circumstances do not determine
our success, there are still fertile and harmful environments in which we
operate. Have you ever wondered how your current environment
supports your development? Let's do a little test. Next to each statement,
choose either yes or no, depending on how well the statement describes
your situation:

Please circle yes or no according to your opinion on each
statement:

Generally speaking, others are ahead of me   Yes / No

My environment challenges me to evolve
   Yes / No

I focus mainly on moving forward   Yes / No

My environment is positive   Yes / No

I am often in my growing area   Yes / No

I wake up in the morning excited about the day   Yes / No

I will not be punished for failure
    Yes / No

Others evolve around me	*Yes / No*
My environment is change-friendly	*Yes / No*
Others assume I'm evolving	*Yes / No*
How many questions did you answer yes to?	________

Your environment will likely support your development if you have six or more 'yes' answers. If you had more 'no' answers, what needs to change in your environment to make it more supportive of your development, and how do you make this change? Also, consider the environment's quality for those questions that are essential to your success.

In this chapter, we looked at your situation from internal and external perspectives. The aim has been to understand and develop your capacity to achieve objectives. We also recognized that managing your time is extremely important to free yourself to do the things you want. We will continue the same theme in the next chapter in more detail and start to put things in order.

Put things in order.

The order in which things are done matters. For example, in most cultures, a multi-course meal is eaten in a particular order. Typically, we start with an appetizer, including a salad, soup, or light starters. Then, we move on to the main course, a more substantial meal of potatoes, meat, fish, or vegetables. And finally, a dessert, which usually consists of an absurd amount of fat and sugar to massage the taste buds in our mouth. Imagine what would happen if we followed the American bumper sticker: *'Life is short, so eat dessert first.'* How many of us would move on from a gourmet cake to a salad, followed by a hearty main course of vegetables? At least the quantity of healthy eating would probably be less. So, for excellent reason, most cultures eat the nutritious part of the meal first and the treats afterward if there is still room in the stomach (although some would insist that there is a separate stomach for dessert). This same principle applies to achieving meaningful goals! If having fun and doing nice things is a priority, then the critical, less entertaining tasks are easily left out or at least progressed less. Influential people organize things differently. They do the difficult but necessary things first, and when they are done, they reward themselves with something nice. For example, I'm going to the cinema tonight, and I've already bought a ticket. But that means I can only go to the cinema if I first meet the goal I set today for writing this chapter. This combination of carrot and stick keeps me focused on rewarding myself with a movie (or if I don't make progress, the stick is to keep writing, skip the film, and lose the ticket). This real threat makes my brain constantly think of the best way to create value for you, my dear reader.

This chapter looks at your life holistically to help you understand the broader priorities. The methods described in this book are very effective and should not be used to pursue the wrong things. Smaller goals (achievable within a six-month timeframe) should always be set about your own broader goals. Otherwise, it is easy to pursue things that do not take you where you want to go. A basis for making your life plan is included in this book. It provides a structure to rethink and update the plans as life progresses. I go through my plan in full once a year and update it with more minor things as needed a few times a year. It doesn't have to be too detailed a plan for your life, but it's a good tool for focusing on the right things. But before we get into the plan, take a moment to think about the following four things:

What does a perfect family life look and feel like for you? Where would you live and with whom? What kind of lifestyle would you have? How would you behave with your family, and how would they behave with you? What kind of things would you do yourself, and what would you do with your family? Who would you like to spend your free time with, and how? How much do you go to church?

What can you do more of and do less to achieve the goals described above?

What does your dream job/study/retirement career look, sound, and feel like? Think about it as broadly as possible and identify the things vital to your work. What kind of things would you do? With whom? What kind of remuneration would you get for it? What would motivate you to get out of bed and go to work every morning?

What should you do more and less to achieve the goals you described above?

3) What would it be like if you had perfect physical and mental health? How would you feel? How would you look? How much would you weigh? How would you dress? How would you walk? What would your posture be like? How much exercise would you do and in what ways? How would you relieve stress? Do you believe in God and the help He offers?

What can you do more of and do less to achieve the goals described above?

What kind of financial situation would you like for yourself and your family? How much money would you have in your current account? How much in savings? How much was invested? How much money would you need to be financially independent? When could you retire? How much would you give to charity?

What can you do more of, and what can you do less of to achieve the financial goals you have described above?

These questions will help you understand what is important to you and what is not. You should spend most of your energy on promoting the things you list above and minimize your energy on things that do not promote them, as this is easily a waste of time! And remember that you are living your own life. Even if you have a spouse, children, and others around you, everyone must still live and advance their lives together. So, double-check that the things you write down are things you want, not things that someone else wants or that others would consider good things. You cannot do a disservice to anyone but yourself.

What gets your heart beating?

The good old Pareto rule (from 1895) has been proven to work so well for over a century that dozens of books have been published to prove its validity. According to Pareto, 20% of people enjoy 80% of the benefits and riches of life. Aiming for that 20% would be best to get more value for your time and effort. This is made possible by understanding who you are, your skills and interests, and, therefore, what order you should put things in in your life. There is no point in spending your time on things that do not contribute to the overall development of your life. And, of course, not everything should always be measured in terms of money alone. Your life plan is essential to know what you want from your life. Unfortunately, very few people take the time to understand themselves and make conscious choices about the direction of their lives. But I know you don't want to be one of those people who wander through life without knowing because you have bought yourself this book.

You may have heard of a motivational speaker called *Simon Sinek*. He became famous through the *Golden Circle* principle[*], which guides

---

[*] https://www.youtube.com/watch?v=qp0HIF3SfI4

people to focus on why, what, and how they should make products in their companies. The original Golden Circle includes:

- **What does the company do?** What are the ten beautiful and good things that products and services do? What do they cost? What do they solve? What do they make easier? What?

- **How does the business work?** How are the products made? How does the company respect the environment?

- **Why does the company exist?** Why do its employees get up in the morning? Why does it tick? Why should people care about the company?

In the words of Simon Sinek: *"People don't buy what a company does; they buy why a company does it."* Although Simon focused on companies, I have also found the principles extremely useful in setting personal priorities. The questions above can be translated into a format that works for you as follows:

- **Why do I want to do what I want to do?** Why am I highly motivated to get this thing done? Why do I persevere in this cause despite any difficulties?

- **What do I need to do to get what I want?** What strengths can I use to make it happen? What are my values that underpin doing this?

- **How can I do this in the best possible way?** When do I need it ready? Who can help me with this? How will I finance this? What risks do I need to manage?

The above order matters. Think about the sentence *'The dog bit John'* and its meaning. If we change the order of the same words, *'John bit the dog,'* *they* will produce a different result, which is also the case in the list above. After years of active use, the tool best guides your life in the order of why, what, and how. I go through the exercise above before I start doing anything. I expect it to take more than a short moment. Doing anything that takes time requires understanding your motivation;

otherwise, it is straightforward to miss the point. And the more substantial the reason, the more likely you will get there.

What things are on your mind? What are you either doing or want to do? Fill in the answers to the above questions for the five things that take up most of your time, and think about how well they still fit in with your current situation and whether you want to change them (such as stopping doing them).

Subject 1

Why?

What?

How?

Subject 2

Why?

What?

How?

Subject 3

Why?

What?

How?

Subject 4

Why?

What?

How?

Subject 5

Why?

What?

How?

Prioritize the above topics for yourself:

1. The most important:

2. The main one:

3. The most important:

4. Most important:

5. The most important

And in the future, focus only on the first few!

Now that you have prioritized a few things, you can move on to making a life plan. There is no right way to do this, and your plan will evolve as you use it. I've been actively using the framework below for over ten years, so it fits my needs. You can use it as a starting point and develop it further to suit your needs.

The life plan consists of eight components:

1. Mission

2. Principles

3. Roles

4. Objectives

5. Work

6. Results

7. Performance indicators

8. Findings

Let's go through each component, and what they are intended to achieve. The mission includes what you want to be and do in life. You can write down the things that are most important to you. Based on previous exercises, you can also write here what life means to you. This is a life-wide description of you and your most important goals at the top level. Everything you do should fit your core purpose and not conflict with it. Here are some examples of famous people's core mission statements that they have shared publicly:

- Oprah Winfrey (TV personality): *To be an inspiring teacher who enables her students to be more than they knew they could be.*

- Elon Musk (entrepreneur): *try anything important enough, even if it could lead to failure.*

- Malala Yousafzai (Nobel laureate): *I want to serve people. And I want every child to get an education.*

- Ai Weiwei (artist): *I want to say something with my art.*

People's primary tasks are as varied as people's. Everyone has a purpose in this world, and so do you. And no one will give you your mission; you must choose it yourself. I aim to be a faithful follower of Jesus and build my treasure in heaven. I also want to be healthy and strong both mentally and physically. In addition, my mission includes a happy family and good friends. You, too, will soon be able to reflect on your mission.

As the name suggests, principles include the principles and rules that are important to you. This section may also include your values if you have defined them. This list should contain your critical beliefs about what you consider valuable, necessary, and acceptable. This can consist of cultural, moral, and religious principles. Why is it vital for you to define them? Because they allow you to focus on the essentials of your life. They help you make choices and decisions. They also help you to become more consistent and coherent in your actions, thoughts, and statements. Again, there is no ready-made list of principles you should choose from. Everyone has their principles, and you probably already know some of them (and can consciously develop them further). Here are examples of some famous people's principles:

- Winston Churchill (politician): *Never gave up.*

- Warren Buffet (billionaire): *honesty is a costly gift; don't expect it from cheap people.*

- Andrew Carnegie (entrepreneur): *wealth is not for boosting our egos but feeding the hungry.*

- Albert Einstein (inventor): *I am passionately curious.*

And of course, they have more than one principle; here are just a few examples. My principles include wanting to love people and God more than possessions, being trustworthy, and helping whenever possible. You, too, will soon get to reflect on your principles.

Who are you to others?

Roles include a maximum of seven different roles you have in your life. According to Stephen R. Covey, people can manage that number of roles but not more. These roles can be anything you are to yourself and other people. For example, my roles are father, husband, friend, co-worker, follower of Jesus, and lifelong learner. You can also define the outcome for each of these roles (what others would say about you about that role), who that role influences around you, and what the fruits of that role are. For example, let's take the role of *a parent*. For this role, you could hope others would say you were *'an exemplary and good parent to your children.'* Naturally, this role will affect both your children and your spouse. The fruits of the parent role could be being present to your children, loving and encouraging them, and *teaching them to know God.* Naturally, your definitions could be very different. You don't have to have seven roles either; you could have fewer. However, I would not recommend taking the Bible's Paul's approach of being all things to all people (unless that is your life mission) as it is very challenging to maintain.

Goals include the dreams that you want to achieve. The main difference between dreams and goals is that your goals have a deadline and a plan to reach them. This can include your biggest goals and aspirations that you intend to achieve. Perhaps you want to pay off your mortgage early or retire younger. Or maybe your goal is to buy a nice car or boat. This may also include goals related to exercise, nutrition, and mental abilities. You determine what your biggest goals in life are.

The **work** component focuses on what you do for a living. If you are studying, this will include the essential things to study. If you are a pensioner, you can use this section to describe how you participate in society and how you spend your everyday life. This section can be broken down into subsections, which include things like people, environment, and what you don't like about your job.

Of course, you can deal with this area in other ways. Here are some examples of my life plan for work:

- People: *working together, colleagues caring about each other, colleagues who know how to do their job, no nasty or lying people.*

- Environment: *work from home at least two days a week, flexible hours, and holidays at least six weeks a year.*

- Focus: *my current work objectives.*

- The undesirable characteristics: *greed, unnecessary meetings and phone calls, long commutes, office politics, too long days.*

You can adapt this section to suit your needs and work.

The **results** section is where you can celebrate the goals you've already achieved. You can record dreams, work accomplished, fitness, and other tasks completed. You can create a photo collage with pictures from your journey. My achievements include academic, spiritual, work-related, and physical successes. And don't worry if your list isn't long or impressive in your own opinion; everyone is a champion of their own life. The more inspired you get with this section, the more it will help you achieve your goals because you know you've already done certain things in your life!

Performance indicators are a forward-looking area where you set yourself targets. Where the results record what you have already achieved, the performance indicator area describes your future goals and related metrics. Keep your performance indicators as specific as possible, as vague goals rarely materialize. I have divided my performance measures into four sub-sections: physical fitness, mental fitness, financial success, and fundamentals. The physical fitness section includes running, fitness, martial arts, and swimming goals. The mental fitness section includes how often I pray, meditate, indulge, eat clean vegetarian food, etc. The financial section includes my net worth, mortgage, and income goals. The basics section includes all my other goals, such as being grateful daily, solving problems immediately, and using positive language when describing things.

The findings are the final element of this model. It contains inspirational quotes from people I admire and hold up as role models. For me, this section also includes several quotes from the Bible that I use as my guide. Here are some examples:

- Philippians 4:6-7: *Do not be anxious about anything, but always bring what you need to God's attention through prayer, petition, and thanksgiving.*

- Denzel Washington (actor): *Ease is a more significant threat to success than difficulty.*

- Navy Seals: the *only easy day was yesterday.*

Of course, my life plan contains more statements than the ones above, but these are examples of statements I can use daily and have special meaning for me. What are the arguments that encourage you to move forward? Write them in the table below.

There are many ways you can put your life plan into practice. You can write them down on paper, draw them as pictures on a blackboard, or make a comic or a collage of images. My life plan is in PowerPoint and printed on the wall with a color printer. I can easily update it with a pencil and reprint individual pages. I leave it to you to decide what works best for you to implement your life plan.

You can now start by writing your thoughts in the box below:

Mission:

Principles:

Roles:

Objectives:

Work:

Results:

Performance
indicators:

Findings:

Life is full of choices, and a life plan helps you to make. However, sometimes situations arise where you have several options (for example, when changing jobs and receiving several job offers). I have developed an Excel file to help you make decisions, which allows you to rank your options according to how important each is to you. As it is challenging to describe this file in a book, here is a lighter version of this technique that you can use:

1. List all your options for making a decision / solving a problem / next step in any issue.

2. Repeat and complete the table below for each option:

   - Write down which things need to happen to select this option. If these things do not occur, this option is not possible.
   - Write down which things must not happen so that you can choose this option. If these things happen, this option is not possible.
   - Write down all the factors that influence this option in a list.
   - Put two numbers next to these things. The first number tells you how important this factor is to you. The second number tells you how likely this factor is to occur in this option. Use a scale of 0 to 10, where 0 means that the thing is not important or likely to happen. Ten is very important to you or very likely to happen.
   - Calculate a score for each contributing factor by multiplying the importance of the factor by its probability (i.e., multiply the numbers of the items in the same row by each other).
   - Add up the scores for all the influencing factors under each option.

3. Compare the scores.

4. Listen to yourself: do you agree with the scores? Are you satisfied with the option with the highest score? Based on these options, what is the right decision in this case?

Here is an example for you to evaluate two jobs:

Option A)   Car rental company Autonyt

This must happen: Holidays 4 weeks a year.

This must not happen:	Long working weeks of more than 50 hours.		
Influencing factors	**Importance**	**Probability**	**Sum**
Nice colleagues	9	7	9 * 7 = 63
Company car	3	0	3 * 0 = 0
Salary 40 000 $	7	8	7 * 8 = 56
Close to home	6	10	6 * 10 = 60
A good reputation	4	3	4 * 3 = 12

TOTAL POINTS: **191**

Option B)	Car rental company Kaarapian		
This must happen:	Holidays 4 weeks a year.		
This must not happen:	Long working weeks of more than 50 hours. It's too long a commute.		
Influencing factors	**Importance**	**Probability**	**Sum**
Nice colleagues	9	6	9 * 6 = 54
Company car	3	0	3 * 0 = 0
Salary 40 000 $	7	6	7 * 6 = 42
Work indoors	6	7	6 * 7 = 42
Free car wash	4	1	4 * 1 = 4

TOTAL POINTS:

In the example above, you can see that Autonyt Car Rental scored better than Carapian. You may also have noticed that the first three contributing factors are the same (and thus have the same importance in both situations) but have different probabilities according to what we have learned earlier from these fictitious employers. The example includes slightly different things to both for the sake of the example because not all jobs are always directly comparable, and so there may be differences in the influencing factors. Now, you would have quantitative and qualitative data to support your decision. And, of course, in this example, you could also have a third option to keep your current job.

Below is a blank table for you to use for your purposes:

Option:

This must happen:

This must not happen:

Influencing factors	**Importance**	**Probability**	**Sum**

TOTAL
POINTS:

The technique above is designed to make complex decision-making more practical by listing each option and the issues that affect it. Scoring then helps you rank the options in order of how important and likely they are to you.

This chapter has looked at different ways of prioritizing. You can use these techniques whenever you need to, and the more you use them, the more natural they will become for you. This brings us to the end of the book's first part, which focuses on building the foundations. You now have many life skills that you can apply as you pursue your dreams.

Part 2. TO HUNDRED

The first part of this book focused on laying the groundwork for the second part, where we'll put our heads together to help you achieve your goals. Most of us do not have a realistic idea of our abilities. Too many people stay just inside their comfort zone, which doesn't compel them to grow and find new and better ways of doing things. Many are plagued by the so-called *"comfort of mediocrity."* And there's nothing wrong with not wanting to go beyond yourself and create even more value in the world if what you have now is enough. However, God created people in his image, and God is the creator of all that is good and beautiful in this world (and even if you are not a believer, you can hardly deny the incredible power and beauty of nature and people, which surpasses all imagination). That power is also within us all, but harnessing it takes focus and action. And that's why so many people fail to fully understand this power: they don't choose any areas to develop or focus enough on advancing those things. Thus, most people do not excel often because they specialize in small, insignificant things instead of more extensive, meaningful actions. But I know you, if anyone, understand this well because you've gotten this book and made it this far! Something inside you is calling out for self-growth and transforming you into what you were created to be: *fully capable and fully aware of your life and its value to yourself and others.* None of us is useless or worthless; most of us could add even more value if we chose.

All of us are created to do something great with our lives, and this idea is comforting. Each of us has our place and time to add value to each other. Within each of us is a gift we can give. The question is, are you unlocking the full potential within yourself? Will you take those challenging but nurturing steps that will lift you to a new level? Or do you keep your candle under a lid, your light away from others? This part of the book focuses on unlocking this power in your chosen area, with the aim that when you go to bed at night, you can say *the day was well spent*. For one, at the end of my life, God willing, I want to say that *this life was as well lived as I could*. Of course, I don't do any of this to please you, God, or myself, but because I had my time in this world, and the better I use it, the more I give to others and myself. Thus, I challenge you to finish reading this book first and then use its advice to make yourself real for at least the next six months. Did you know that 80% of the books people buy are never read? We do things differently; we take responsibility for our lives and do something with it.

In the first part, the order of the chapters did not matter, as they all set the scene for the following process that consists of these six steps:

- Plan your way to success.

- Start where you are.

- Do enough of the right things.

- Assess progress and development.

- Work towards the goal and enjoy the journey.

- Reset and move on to new adventures.

Each of these contains practical guidance on planning and implementing the objectives you want to achieve. This process is not just about getting things done and moving forward but a journey to grow and achieve your goals. Everyone would do it if it were easy, but many miss that such challenging goals give you satisfaction along the way, even if you don't get there. Just repeatedly pushing yourself beyond your limits will boost your self-esteem. And for these changes to have real value, they must be sustainable. We've all tried new diets, fitness programs, and other things that have brought temporary benefits. Many have been attempting these so often that we have already lost faith in lasting change. So, we need to think differently:

- ***Raise your expectations of yourself.*** Albert Einstein said it's crazy to do the same thing repeatedly and expect different results. It would be best to change your mindset about what you expect from yourself in the future. This includes the things you want in your life and those you don't want. Without internal change, it is pointless to expect lasting external results.

- *Change your own beliefs.* It's not enough to change your expectations if you don't believe you can achieve them. For example, if you expect to become a millionaire without believing you can make that much money, expecting it ever to happen is pointless. So, changing your beliefs about who you are and what is possible for you would be best.

- *Change the way you do things.* Identify the things that move you towards your goals and the things that stop you from achieving them. Then, reinforce the supporting behaviors and remove the weakening ones. Remember that big rivers flow from small streams, and so will your results.

Now you have the treasure map of your life in your hands, but you are the one who must go on this adventure and find the treasure. And believe me, you were made to do this!

So, let's start with the first step, planning the road to success.

Plan your way to success.

Imagine you see a mountain in front of you, a mighty grey rock wall that rises out of sight. It would be best if you were miles away to see its massive size and height in full. This majestic sight has an impressive name, *El Capitan* - The Captain. Indeed, this captain commands the challenge, which is why it is one of the world's most famous accessible climbing destinations. Located in Yosemite National Park, the wall is half a mile in height, with several sections with an outward curve and very flat spots with nothing to grab onto except for a few grains of rock. If you had been at the foot of El Capitan on 3 June 2017 and had a powerful telescope with you, you would have been able to see the red dot on the face of the mountain. It would have been *Alex Honnold*, the world's most successful free climber and the only person to have successfully climbed the El Capitan without any safety equipment. *Dozens of others who have attempted the same feat now lie flat in the graveyard.* And the hundreds of others who have climbed this wall have been fully equipped for several days. For a good reason, Alex's feat is considered one of the most outstanding sporting achievements ever. Watch the Free Solo documentary film, which shares Alex's biography and achievements to see this yourself. What's interesting for us is how Alex planned and prepared for the challenge. He had only one main goal: to climb to the El Capitan's peak alive, without any tools or aid. All the other things he had to do were sub-goals to that end (and that trip included several other of the best climbs in the world). Alex learned every detail of the Capitan's route, down to the last hole and crevice. He wrote them down in detail in his climbing diary. He climbed the route (with a safety harness) continuously and visualized the route in his mind every day. He climbed most of the route without a safety harness in short sections (except for one section that required a jump and was so dangerous to do without any safety that Alex did not try it even once beforehand without equipment). Throughout this time, Alex lived in a small caravan at the foot of the Capitan to always see his challenger. Alex had a small wooden pole at the door of the caravan, which he hung by his bare fingers for hours each day. He was dedicated to the goal. And his journey was not without its complications. Alex almost died several times while training, and, just the day before, he fell from a height of about 100 feet while training on the Capitan, but luckily, he had his safety gear on. Alex says he would not have succeeded in this almost unattainable goal without thorough, detailed planning and training.

What's the point in planning, as life happens anyway?

Comprehensive planning of one's life is rare today, even though most have a calendar and diary. Mark McCormack (from Harvard Business

School) has researched that only 3% of people have written down their goals and plans and follow them. His research shows that these 3% are more successful than the other 97% combined. Please do your survey and ask some people you know how many of them have an up-to-date life plan to show. I asked dozens of my acquaintances, and none had one (and none were planning to). I've been making annual plans for the last ten years because my mentors John C. Maxwell and Tony Robbins recommended it. I fully update my life plan once a year and make more minor updates as needed throughout the year. I printed it on my wall to remind me what I want to invest my time in. And why is such a plan so important? *It's hard to get where you want if you have no idea how you will get there. For* most people, goals and desires constantly change and can never reach a moving target. So, you must think about, choose, and lock in your goals to get there. This reduces the risk of getting sidetracked and wasting time that does not take you in the desired direction. *People with clear goals are more successful because they are more focused.* Be careful because most of us say we already have goals. The pity is that they are mostly just hopes and dreams because they are usually backed up by a lack of both a plan and action. This whole book's message is right at its heart: *how to focus your actions to achieve your defined goals.* Those who lack this plan start doing something else entirely as soon as there is any resistance to progress. So, *you need to define your goals as clearly as possible, plan how you will get there, and then move forward with your plan every day.* The detailed planning process is so helpful that even if you don't even take a step to advance your action plan, it still develops your brain (i.e., creates new neuropaths). This plan becomes an internal prompting voice that guides and reminds you of its very existence: you will automatically start doing more things in your plan because your brain needs it to carry out the plan. So why don't people plan and set goals for themselves more? Some of the most common reasons include the following:

- *They do not attach importance to plans and targets.* They have missed that the ability to set goals is more critical to their success than anything else. Studies show that people of average intelligence who plan a lot are significantly more successful than those of top intelligence who do not plan. What is your attitude towards planning your life? And now that you think about it, how has it affected your success so far?

- ♦ *They don't know how to plan.* This is true for many people. Many people think that worries and vain hopes such as *"I want to be rich"* or *"I want to be happy"* are planned. The only thing such phrases do is mislead customers. Plans should focus on specific, well-defined goals and include clear steps. We'll go through some easy techniques for doing this in a moment.

- ♦ *They are afraid of failing.* Failure hurts until you realize there is no such thing as failure, as all experiences are good for learning. Either they lead us towards our goals, or they teach us how not to reach them. I never tire of quoting Thomas Edison: I have not failed; I have learned over a thousand *ways to make a light bulb not work*. It is useless cowardice not to set goals for yourself for fear of failing. But after sufficient planning or evaluation, you can make a conscious decision not to do something if, for some reason, it doesn't pay off.

- ♦ *They are afraid of being criticized.* Many people think: *What if I set a goal and don't reach it? What if my plan doesn't work?* And that others will laugh, *"I told you it wouldn't work out."* And it is possible that your plans and goals must be changed along the way. If you are unsure about your progress or dedication, you can keep your goals and plans to yourself and let others draw their conclusions based on your results. Or you can limit the sharing of information to your chosen accountability partners. It is also good to remember that if your goals and plans change, you do not need to tell yourself or others that you failed but that you changed your goals to suit your situation better, which everyone would understand.

In 2006, *USA Today* magazine published an article looking at people who had made New Year's resolutions. About 4% of those who had only made their promises verbally rather than writing them down had managed to keep them over the next 12 months. In comparison, 44% of those who had written down their promises had kept them! That's a dramatic difference in results. Of course, it doesn't mean that simply writing down your goals guarantees success, but rather that *setting clear goals and writing them down increases your chances of success tenfold. The* Greek philosopher *Aristotle did* not say in vain that people are goal-oriented; some are more than others.

Well planned is half done, or is it?

The old Finnish saying that *well-planned is half-done* still holds. Sure, you can make perfect plans on how to get something done, but you won't get results if you don't execute your plans. Therefore, perhaps the meaning of the saying is that you shouldn't rush into things because the result may be worse than if you had done nothing. I learned this the hard way in three start-ups with my friends. We had great ideas about delivering value to customers, but in all of them, we hit a wall within a year or two because we hadn't considered all the factors that contribute to success at a sufficient level. In some companies, we underestimated the need for early funding and ran out of money. In others, we were carried away by our enthusiasm and lacked skills in sales and marketing. This is why long-term planning is vital for success, to avoid the harmful effects of short-termism.

The inventor of car mass production, *Henry Ford,* believed that even the most significant goals can be achieved if you break them down into small enough steps. As they say, eating an elephant one piece at a time is possible. If you want to achieve a big goal, you can break it down into smaller steps that are easier:

> Happiness comes from the pursuit of an important idea or goal.

- List all the challenges and difficulties you may encounter on your way to your goal. Write down internal and external challenges, i.e., those that may haunt you or others. Consider any changing circumstances (for example, if your goal is to make a certain amount of money, how might a recession or a situation like the interest rate crisis affect that)? Make the list as long as you can. Then, put another column next to it and write down what you can do to avoid potential challenges in advance.

- List all the knowledge and skills you need to achieve your goal. For example, suppose you want to run a marathon within a specific time limit. In that case, you need to learn techniques, training, nutrition management, recovery, and many other things to make the actual task of running possible. Think beyond the goal; think about the needed knowledge and skills. Of course, this list will need constant updating as things progress, as your understanding of what is required grows, and the information becomes outdated quickly.

- List who can help you reach your goal. Who can support you, who might be able to do some of the work, and who you can ask for advice? Humans were not created to work alone (even Adam in the Bible had God as his mentor, Eve as his helper, and, unfortunately, the Devil as his boss).

- List all the things you need to do and be responsible for. This first part of your plan will help you to see what kind of job you have ahead of you.

Millionaire and one of the wealthiest men of his time, *H.L. Hunt*, said the secrets of his success were three requirements. The first is that you decide precisely what *you want* out of life, the second is knowing the price you must pay, and the third and most important is paying *the price. In* practical terms, this means that whatever you want out of life, it should be worth it to do what it takes to achieve it. It is easy to make promises and decisions and start contributing to their progress. But with any goal worth pursuing, there comes a time somewhere along the way when progress becomes difficult or a wall. This is when you measure how much you want to get there, not just get stuck along the way. We all want to be successful, but not all of us are willing to pay the price it takes to get there. And that's okay; according to Pareto's rule, 80% of those who fail fall into the group that only gets 20% of the results on offer. *For them, excuses take the prize instead of achieving the goal, especially* when the price of success must be paid in full and in advance! *Zig Ziglar* (the American salesman) aptly said that ***the elevator to success is permanently broken, but the stairs are always available.***

Warren Buffet has given simple (but not easy) three steps on how to turn your dreams into reality:

1. Know what you want.

2. Get the tools, knowledge, experience, and skills you need, and use them to get what you want.

3. Focus carefully on the previous two.

Warren knows what he's talking about, given that he's been one of the wealthiest people in the world for a long time. In addition to the above wisdom, he has given us five steps to set our priorities:

1. List all the things you want in your life.

2. Choose the Top 25 things you want more in your life than any other.

3. Choose the Top 5 you will start thinking about in more depth.

4. Make an initial action plan for these Top 5 things.

5. Make a list of things you avoid at all costs. And what goes on that list? All the things you didn't choose for your Top 5!

6. Choose the one you really want to focus on now and use the lessons in this book to help you achieve that goal*.

Maybe the fifth step surprised you? The fact is that people can only do one thing at a time and many in a row. So, too many things to do takes time and attention away from those that could be best spent on them. So don't spend your time on things, not on your Top 5 list. I also have my own Top List printed on my wall so I can see it daily and remember to ask myself how what I'm doing today contributes to my most important goals (for example, writing this book contributes to my goal of helping others).

Let's make the following Top 20 list for you. You can first list all the things you want to achieve, and if it's longer than 20 things, then you can choose the most important ones for this list:

---

* The author's addition of a sixth step, which Warren left off his own list...

Some people may have a hundred ideas about what they want to achieve, while others may have an empty list, which is understandable as we are at different points in our lives. In case you fall into the relatively *empty list* category, here are some questions to help you think about what might be on your list:

- What kind of things make you happy?

- What things do others praise and thank you for doing?

- What are you good at / talented at / accomplished at?

- What things would you like to spend a lot of time doing?

- Imagine you won the jackpot in the Lottery six months ago. What kind of things would you be doing right now?

- What things would you do if you knew you wouldn't fail at any of them?

- If you could do anything in the world, what would it be?

- What are the things that most need fixing in this world?

- Where would other people benefit most from your help?

- What kind of books do you like? What could you do based on them?

- What would be your dream job or hobby?

- What would you like to be remembered for?

- What are the things that interest you most?

- What kind of revolution would you like to lead?

Once you have your Top 20 list, the next step is to find your Top 5 list. You can start by putting the number 1 next to the first target. Then, look at the next target on the list. If it's more important than the first one, move the number 1 next to it. Then, move on to the third and compare whether it is more important than where number 1 is currently. If so, move the number 1 next to it. Go through the whole list until number 1 is next to the goal that is most important to you on the list. Now put number 2 next to the first goal on the list and go through the same process (obviously skipping the one that already has number 1). Repeat this process until you have the five most essential goals selected. List them here:

My top 5 list:

1.

2.

3.

4.

5.

Now list the 15 goals that missed the Top 5. Don't *waste your time on the* list:

> *I don't waste my time on these things:*
>
> ❖
> ❖
> ❖
> ❖
> ❖
> ❖
> ❖
> ❖
> ❖
> ❖
> ❖
> ❖
> ❖
> ❖
> ❖

Next, make an initial action plan to achieve the five objectives. Then, choose the one you want to focus on. It would be best if you now had chosen the goal you want to focus on for the next six months (or whatever the appropriate timeframe is; more on that later in Part 3 of the book).

Daddy, are we there yet?

Once you understand your goal, the first step in planning is to develop a list of things you could do to advance it. The list can be divided into categories according to what can be done now, soon, and in the future. This book uses a six-month timeline (it can also be any other timeline you prefer), so you can develop ideas for what you can do immediately, four months from now, and six months from now. Also, write down what each thing will achieve and think about how it would contribute to achieving your goal. At this planning stage, you don't need to think about accessibility; we'll do that later. The idea is to list and sequence the tasks.

Objective:

First month	2-4 months	4-6 months
Things you could do in a month (and how they will help you achieve your goal)	Things you could do in 2-4 months (and how they will help you achieve your goal)	Things you could do within 4-6 months (and how they contribute to your goal)

The table above sets out an indicative order of priority for the tasks to be carried out and sequences them over time. Most likely, the details will decrease the longer you think about things over a more extended period. The aim is not to create a precise six-month project plan but to understand what needs to happen over the next few months.

Defining these tasks is worth using the already well-known SMART method (which is also an abbreviation of the word). The main advantage of tasks and milestones written in SMART is that they are easy to understand and measure once implemented. SMART target comes from the words:

- *S = Clearly defined: the* objective must be unambiguously understood and sufficiently precise to say whether it has been achieved. For example, a clearly defined goal would be "I will run a half marathon." An ambiguously defined goal would be "run a long distance."

- *M = Measurable:* the target must have clear achievement indicators showing whether you have reached this target. For example, a measurable goal would be to "run a half marathon in under two hours." A poorly quantifiable goal would be to "run a long distance in a few hours."

- *A = Achievable:* this is important to assess to ensure that the target continues supporting the goals you want to achieve. It is not worth doing if a task or sub-goal does not directly contribute to the primary goal.

- *R = Realistic:* This is where you assess how feasible it is to achieve this goal based on the previous three points and your situation. If your goal is not realistically achievable for you, you need to consider how to measure and time the goal to make it possible. If you haven't run in the last six months, running a marathon in three months is not realistic. So, in this example, you would extend your training schedule to get more miles on your feet.

- *T = Time-bound: the* target must also have a timetable. You will recall from earlier that the difference between a dream and a goal is the achievement date. For example, a clearly defined, measurable, and time-bound goal would be "I will run a half marathon in under two hours within the next six months." A poorly defined goal would be to "run a long distance in a few hours within the next few months."

To help you define SMART objectives and tasks, the following supporting questions are provided:

- What needs to change to reach your main goal?

- Who is involved in this issue? Who can support and help you?

- What is your starting point?

- What is the desired outcome?

- By when do you need to reach the desired outcome?

- How do you know that the sub-objective directly supports your main objectives?

- Where and how do you monitor the achievement of the target?

Some of your goals, such as the abovementioned running goal, may be very short. Some goals may require a much longer description to make them more transparent. Here are some more examples of SMART goals for different areas of life:

- I sell at least $ 20,000 worth of X products per month, every month (assuming that the main objective is to secure my own sales commission).

- I will increase customer satisfaction with the NPS to at least 50 by May next year (assuming the main objective is improving the customer experience).

- I will eat a minimum of 1,500 and a maximum of 2,000 kilocalories daily for the next six months (assuming the main goal is to lose a certain amount of weight).

- I focus on my work in 50-minute work periods and 10-minute breaks for 8 hours a day, five days a week (assuming that the main objective is to improve my work efficiency).

- I will learn to program a Python-based worm game within the next three months (assuming the goal is to learn a new programming language).

- I will give a speech at three different events over the next three months and record them on video, which I will analyze after each speech to identify areas for improvement (assuming the aim is to improve my public speaking skills).

The examples above give you an indication of the main and sub-goals you can set for yourself. The main difference between primary and sub-goals is the level of detail and scale of the goals (*for example, a primary goal might say what you want to achieve in the next six months, while a sub-goal might focus first on one month, then another sub-goal on one week, and other sub-goals on each day*). You can see more examples of how to set a primary goal and break it down into sub-goals through the programs at the end of the book.

> *Go through the list of objectives you wrote earlier and write down the tasks and sub-objectives using the SMART technique:*

Goals like the ones described above are essential motivators and directional tools that help you plan how to get to the outcome you want and how to prioritize. For most of us, meeting our goals brings happiness and joy. However, reaching our goals can sometimes feel very far away, leading to frustration. So, it's also good to remind ourselves of the importance of the journey and not just getting there. All experiences are good and teach us. The outcome is what we receive by meeting our goals, and the journey is how we get there. For example:

- If you're a *hockey coach*, perhaps the outcome you want is a world championship team, and how you get there is by finding the right players and assistant coaches and developing ways for your team to win.

♦ If you are *a visual artist*, the desired result could be a new work of art. The journey involves getting paint and canvas and developing the vision and approach needed for the finished artwork.

♦ If you are a *runner*, your goal may be to win a marathon, and your policy is to practice running and fitness every day and ensure you recover adequately.

♦ If you are a *pensioner* managing a charity knitting club, your goal might be to finish 500 woolen hats for kids, and the approach is to get other pensioners to join you in knitting.

What would happen if you forgot your goals and focused solely on improving your practices in specific areas of your choice? Perhaps you would still achieve your goals because it is possible to achieve them with the proper practices. This book is about developing your habits (thinking, beliefs, habits, etc.) rather than just setting goals. One of the pre-readers of the book asked me why the book does not provide more ready-made programs. I said that I could easily make a thick book of ready-made programs, but how would I know that they would start you off on the right foot and lead to the outcome you want, on top of following an action plan you could complete? One size does not fit all, so only you know where you want to get to, where to start, and the most viable route. Sure, it takes some effort, but I don't think you would have been interested in a book like this in the first place if it was a big problem for you. As in any match, you need more points than your opponent, which varies with each game. So, make a plan of action to get you there, and use the goals as a guide!

Your action plan can contain targets that look from the outside in or from the inside out. Our outward-looking goals include weight loss, writing a book, winning a sports competition, and other visible activities. On the inside are things that relate to our being and our fundamental nature, such as how we see the world, treat others, think about ourselves, and what beliefs we hold. Between the two are the behaviors that shape both our external and internal goals. For example, winning a sports competition after many months of training boosts our self-esteem. Similarly, developing our compassion for others leads us, for example, to knit woolen hats for children for many months and send them to Africa. This is also why you can design your own goals to speak in a way that is meaningful to you. If winning a race motivates you, focus on that; if helping others does, then focus on that. There are many ways to achieve the same outcome for many different reasons. Understanding this opened concretely when I read a study on why people run. Of course, many people run to improve their health and fitness, as I assumed they would, but most people run for hundreds of different reasons. For example, someone ran the same race as me because her grandmother had cancer. It is a mystery how the grandmother, or her cancer situation, benefited from that run. Still, the main thing is that everyone finds reasons for fulfilling their goals and following meaningful aspirations. What can understanding this mindset do for you? Let's consider smokers, for example. Let's imagine that two of your friends said they want to quit smoking, and you offer them both a joint. One says *no thanks, I'm trying to quit smoking,* and the other says *no thanks, I'm no longer a smoker.* Which of these persons do you think is more likely to succeed? The same goes for people who want to lose weight: if they say, *"I'm trying to lose weight,"* instead of *"I'm getting to my optimal weight,"* the former is less likely to succeed. This may sound like a slight difference, but there is a link between the outcome and the process and an unhelpful process will not get you there, and a helpful one might. What are your aspirations? Are you learning to play the piano or becoming a pianist? Are you training to run a marathon or becoming an endurance runner? You choose!

During this chapter, it has become clearer what you want to achieve and why. This will allow you to move on to the next step, starting from where you are.

Start where you are

Very few people have everything they need to reach challenging targets straight away. Sure, if you set low enough targets, you can make do with what you already have, but such targets are rarely inspiring enough to achieve a significant milestone. You can use what you already have, whether rich or poor, sick or healthy, tall or short, thin or fat. In practice, you always start where you are and must do and acquire whatever it takes to reach your goals. Thomas Stanley and William Danko interviewed more than 11,000 people over 25 years who have created a million-dollar fortune themselves (they didn't inherit, win, or otherwise get their fortune "for free"). Their main research question was what had made these people become millionaires when most other people find it challenging to get so far from the same starting point. What do you think 85% of millionaires gave as the reason why they became more successful than others who started from the same humble beginnings? They answered: *"I didn't have a better education, greater intelligence, or a bigger nest egg than anyone else, BUT I was willing to do things more than anyone else."* Some are indeed born with a golden spoon in their mouths, and few get unimaginably lucky in the lottery. For the rest of us, there is only one real option for significant success: hard work to advance the right causes. And therein lies the great *secret of* success: **you must start and do things to get there!** I find this very comforting but sad at the same time because there is no guaranteed shortcut to happiness (remember what Zig Ziglar said about this earlier). What about you? Is your focus on doing enough of the right things to join the 20% who take 80% of the results? In the end, it's your choice. Once you've said YES, the self-development discussed earlier and meaningful goals will keep you on that narrow path to success.

But success should not be pursued in unsustainable or self-centered ways. The Bible urges us to seek the kingdom of God (Matthew 6:33). My life started well with a family that had money because my parents had a successful logistics business. But the great recession of the 1990s did its work, and the company went under, and yet the debts remained. My father paid for them for the rest of his life, both financially and emotionally. Although I never lived in straight poverty, I learned from a very young age that money comes and goes and that it is up to you where you end up as circumstances change. Unfortunately, I also learned that achieving your goals by any means and at the expense of others is not worth it. So, it's not just where you get to but how you get there that matters. Some of the bad decisions I made as a young person caused great pain for my family and the community in which I lived. I imagined that unhealthy actions would help me reach my goals more quickly, but I didn't fully understand then that short-term achievements at any cost would have significant negative results in the long run. Once I learned this profoundly important principle, I began to steer my life into paths that would produce long-term results so that I could also be proud of how I achieved them. It has also motivated me to write this book to help you both define the goals that are important to you and achieve them sustainably. As we have already discussed, time is the greatest equalizer in the world. Everyone has 24 hours a day, for as many days as each person happens to live on this earth before our *Heavenly Father* calls us back from this world. And that time can be used well or poorly. So, none of us have enough time to wait for that *one day* that might be better to pursue our dreams than today. The best time and place to start is right where you are now. ***Procrastination is not an option!***

There's still time tomorrow...

We are all familiar with schoolwork and waited so long for it to be done that the neighbor's dog ate it when the teacher asked for it. Besides the dog, many of us are also on a diet that produces neither results nor actions. *We are all sadly familiar with the practice of procrastinating.* Willpower and self-discipline are the tools against procrastinating, along with a good action plan. It would be best to have them, especially when you don't feel like progressing toward your goals or when circumstances try to push you in the other direction with their challenges. Don't be a victim; be responsible for your goals and use self-discipline to focus your energy on the right things. Many people do themselves a disservice by trying to force themselves to do great things, and the resistance eventually becomes insurmountable. But people *thinking fast* focus on the moment and that small resistance in mind. My running development didn't take off until I said out loud, *"I'm going to run my training program, rain or shine."* Consequently, I've ended up running at -22 Fahrenheit in Finland, in total downpours in England (I took a shower to dry myself off when I got home), and at +104 Fahrenheit in West Africa in knee-deep sand. But if I had thought about what to do for that little sentence, my self-discipline would have failed in that moment. Luckily, all I need to do is get myself out right now and take the next step, and once I've taken a step, I'll take the next one. And so, less than two hours later, I've traversed twenty miles of sandy savannah. You can do the same! How aware are you of the dragging of your feet? Let's do a test.

Circle your current situation for each statement:

Procrastination test	Very rarely	Rarely	Sometimes	Often	Very often
I'm pushing to get things done for as long as possible	1	2	3	4	5
I often regret not starting earlier	1	2	3	4	5
I have things I know I should do, but I haven't started yet	1	2	3	4	5
I leave things so last minute that	1	2	3	4	5

I must do them in a hurry					
I know I could have used my time better	1	2	3	4	5
I do many things at the same time	1	2	3	4	5
I get things done when they need to be done*	5	4	3	2	1
I do the most essential things first*	5	4	3	2	1
I use my time wisely*	5	4	3	2	1

COUNT THE
TOTAL OF
THE CIRCLED
POINTS FOR
EACH ROW:

Note that the scores for the last three questions are reversed.

How many points did you get? The list below shows what other people have scored according to the surveys and what kind of procrastinator you are:

- ♦ *19 points or less:* you are in the bottom 10%. Very likely, one of your principles is to do the most important things first.

- ♦ *20-23 points:* about 10-25% of people are in the same group as you. You are still a relatively effective player.

- ♦ *24-31 points:* you belong in the middle. You're a very typical achiever.

- ♦ *32-36 points:* about 10-25% of people are in the same group of high procrastination as you.

- ♦ *37 points or more:* you're in the top 10% of procrastinators. You are known for your style of doing things tomorrow.

We are all familiar with all kinds of things waiting to be done. How many things are you currently waiting to do? Put a check in the boxes that apply to you:

- ☐ Laundry unwashed

- ☐ Dishes not washed or dishwasher not emptied

- ☐ Floors without vacuuming or wiping

- ☐ Holiday plans not made or at least not booked

- ☐ Birthday and Christmas presents not bought

- ☐ Hour logs not filled in at work

- ☐ Lawn not cut or snow plowing not done

- ☐ Difficult conversations unfinished with some people

- ☐ Windows to be washed for this year

- ☐ Unfinished schoolwork

- ☐ Unpaid or unopened invoices

- ☐ Car tire pressures not checked for a year or more

- ☐ Investment plan not made or updated

☐ Other unfinished tasks:

I could go on with the list above, and I bet it would just add more things you should have done already. So, for most people, procrastination is a daily issue and the most well-known enemy of achieving one's goals. Most of the time, the difference with others comes not in the action plan phase but in the implementation phase. For many, the plan remains just an idea without any meaningful action. It is challenging to take the first step and get going. So, in most cases, it is not worth trying to focus on the whole journey and getting to the finish line but on getting things moving. Many people have good intentions to start or continue working towards their goals tomorrow, next weekend, or next week. But other things seem more important when the time comes, so the schedule moves forward again. That's how winter tires are not changed until the first snow has fallen or you've slipped off the road. Impulsiveness (i.e., doing things on the spur of the moment that bring immediate pleasure) takes the edge off longer-term goals that bring pleasure only later. So, what are the things that research shows people are most drawn to? Here are the statistics:

- *Work and career-related issues:* asking for a pay rise, changing, or getting a job. Up to 57% of people say this is their biggest pet peeve.

- *Health-related issues:* exercise, diet, taking medicines, and getting treatment, about 42% of people say this is one of their biggest pet peeves.

- *Financial issues:* saving, investing, and managing your finances. 36% of people say they struggle in this area all the time.

89% of people say they have significant problems in at least one of the three areas described above, and 9% say they have significant challenges in all three areas. It's statistically likely that you could achieve more by reducing your procrastination. A vital belief you should maintain is faith in yourself. Usually, people start to procrastinate as soon as their belief in their ability to finish starts to crack. Please focus on the steps to get there rather than the finish line itself. That way, fatigue doesn't get the better of you before you get there.

Make sure your goals are ambitious enough that you will certainly have to push yourself to reach them. Your starting point can almost look like you're looking at Mount Everest without climbing a single step. It indeed takes courage. And courage is primarily needed to take that first step, even if you can't see the whole path to the end and know you're bound to stumble along the way. It requires conscious patience with yourself and your action plan to reach your goals. When I started running, I never imagined it would also teach me about life. I read in a book by a Navy Seal, now ultramarathoner David Goggins, that when he runs long distances, sometimes he needs to focus on the next step to continue his painful journey. I tried this when setting my running records and found it to be a working mindset. Later, I realized that the same works for other aspects of my life. I, and by extension, you, need to take the next step on the path we have determined will get us there. Whether we get there or not, we grow because we are constantly outdoing ourselves and doing things we never imagined. This builds self-esteem, which, in turn, reduces drag.

Speaking of visualization, one fundamental technique that you can use while sitting on your couch (whatever your goal) is visualization. Finnish Formula 1 celebrities such as Mika Häkkinen and Kimi Räikkönen and many others use visualization to prepare themselves. Several studies have proven through brain imaging that simply imagining doing things builds new neural connections in the brain. For example, one study selected people who could not play the piano. They were put in the same piano lessons to learn to play. In the group, some participants did not visualize, and some did. Those who practiced visualization regularly learned to play the piano faster and more accurately than those who did not. Similarly, formula racers, musicians, artists, students, business leaders, retired people, and anyone else can use visualization to improve their performance and learning abilities. There are many good books on visualization and how to use it, so I'll give you a practical guide to get you started immediately. Maybe this will be your first practical step toward your goal. Follow these steps and develop them into something that works well for you:

1. Find a suitable quiet place where you can make yourself comfortable. Perhaps lie on your bed or sit on your sofa at home. But beware of overly distracting elements around you, such as noisy children, a snoring spouse, or a loud television.

2. Close your eyes. Take a deep breath. With each breath, feel your belly expand and contract. Inhale five or more times: inhale rapidly for 4 seconds, hold your breath for 7 seconds, exhale slowly for 8 seconds, and repeat the process. The timing doesn't have to be precisely that many seconds; the idea is more like taking a quick inhale, holding your breath, and exhaling slowly (and this last step should be the longest). The purpose of this exercise is to oxygenate your brain.

3. Even out your breathing and start to see your goals in your mind. Picture it as vividly as possible and add as much detail as possible as if you were watching a film about your achievement. See yourself as the main character in the film, an active participant. In this film, everything goes exactly as planned, and you get everything you wanted in your goal. You can imagine how you got there, who helped you, what you did. In the same way, you can also enjoy the result of your work and what it gives you and makes you feel.

4. See your current situation in your mind. For example, if your goal is to reach your ideal weight, visualize your current weight. Feel and see your current situation as it is, and focus on the difference between what you want and your current situation. Imagine how your current situation prevents you from achieving your goal and how you must immediately take the following steps to move towards your dream.

5. Imagine your next steps towards your goal as clearly as possible. What will you do? How will you do it? Who will help? How will you help? What will you do to make it possible? What challenges might you face along the way and how will you overcome them? What do you do when your enthusiasm wanes? What do you do when your tools break down? What do you do when others resist? Imagine the next step in your action plan as clearly as possible and see yourself doing it.

6. Get up from your comfortable position and get down to business. Now, you have a vivid picture of what you want, where you are, and what you need to do to move forward. Your brain is fully prepared to make that vision a reality.

This chapter of the book is short and to the point but very important. Many people put off starting too long when they could start by taking things one step at a time. So be different and start today with the first step towards your goal! Suppose you have severe challenges in focusing on the right things (due to addictions, lack of concentration, or other reasons). In that case, it's worth structuring your life to eliminate distractions and timewasters and make procrastination as tricky as possible for yourself. At the same time, you can put things in place that make it as easy as possible to focus on the right things and get things done. And that brings us to the next chapter, where we'll continue discussing doing the right things to advance your goals.

Do enough of the right things

The Bible says *you reap what you sow*. This is a fundamental principle in the book because there is a consequence for every action. I remember philosophy classes in high school and later in college where the meaning and existence of right and wrong were discussed. The theoretical lectures failed to open my eyes significantly to the vital sense of philosophy, nearly as well as the painful and rewarding life experiences.

Quite simply, whenever we say or do something, something follows. When I paid enough attention to this simple fact, my thinking changed. Instead of dwelling on what happened, why things went wrong, or how circumstances were against (or for) me, I began to analyze the decisions and actions that led to this situation. This made me feel better and made it quicker to understand why things had gone the way they had. The change in mindset has helped me to change my approach to understanding the priorities and to modify the paths I have already chosen as necessary. The simple question is: *"What can come of doing this?"* opens the brain to think objectively and to explore different alternative consequences. This, in turn, makes it easier to make decisions and manage risks. Making significant and difficult decisions is made much easier when you know that you have made the best possible decision based on the information available at the time. Of course, time may show some info missing and circumstances changing, but you will never again have to blame yourself for decisions you have made using this way of thinking (because it was the best decision you could make at the time). ***Huh, what a relief to know that at any given moment, you are doing the right thing*** until new information comes along to make a different decision!

Your direction, your results, and your destiny in life are the sum of three things:

- It's up to you to decide what you focus on and how you spend your time. Energy is spent on the things you think about, so the more valuable things you focus on, the more positive results you will get.

- It's up to you to decide what you believe in and what things mean to you. You always have the choice to be a victim or to take responsibility and give things a better meaning.

- Your decision on what you do to achieve your goals. There are no results without action.

These are your own decisions, and your life will reflect their results. So, if you want better results, you must make better decisions. And that doesn't mean that you must make precisely the right decisions all the time, in every situation. It just means making conscious choices about what you spend your life on rather than going with the flow of life, seduced by others.

What time and money have in common is that both can be consumed. However, time is very different from cash because it is never recoverable. Money can be earned, but time cannot. So we can't think about how to get more time, but how best to spend it. Therefore, while trying to save and earn money, we are trying to spend time in the best possible way. Often, people think the other way around: how to spend money and save time, but that is not helpful thinking. Procrastination is the worst possible waste of time because all the wasted time is lost forever. So, you need to be able to assess the value of the time you spend, whether you are wasting it or contributing to your life. Unfortunately, many things we do are on the waste side, requiring self-improvement to focus time on the right things.

There is an interesting discussion in the Bible about the connection between actions and words in faith*. James is evident when he says that there is no faith without works. The same applies to time management. It doesn't matter what you tell others about the importance of things in your life if your actions speak otherwise. Many say work is essential to them, but their evenings are spent watching TV. Others say that family is most important to them, but time is spent at work, at dinner parties, and golf rounds. The actual order of priorities is reflected in everyone's time. If you want to get to know someone, look at how they spend their time. It is, therefore, essential to define what is important to you and then keep to your actions and time management. Sometimes, this requires considerable self-discipline in situations where wasting time is much more tempting than doing the right things. Ultimately, time management is also about understanding a simple cause-and-effect

---

* James 2:14-18: "What good is it, my brother, if someone says he has faith but has no works? Surely faith cannot save him. Someone may say: "You have faith, and I have works"; show me your faith without works, and I will show you faith by my works.

relationship. What is the long-term consequence of what I do? For example, if I sit in the break room chatting away and drinking coffee, I don't have much left after the activity. But if I'm drinking coffee and using my influencing skills to coach a colleague, it's time well spent. Again, this is a conscious choice of how I want to spend time with him. You have the same power over your own time.

Managing your own time is something that many people talk about, and few do. Sure, we all have lots of tools for time management, such as calendars, to-do lists, and bosses and colleagues telling us how to spend our time. However, how we choose to spend our time is not only logical but also intensely emotional. This is why purely logic-based time management methods are bound to fail somewhere along the line: emotions easily take over in people. Everyone knows what they should be doing, but they do something else because it is more emotionally satisfying. So essential but unpleasant tasks are easily left at the bottom of the pond. The traditional two-dimensional order of priorities involves two things: *importance and urgency*. This is an attempt to make two very emotional things logical because what is important or urgent to one person is not necessarily so to another. This approach (or any other) does not add hours to the day but moves less critical things to the bottom of the list. So, the tool has limited utility. But should we then try to do things faster or more? That's how the world looks these days from both *#demandeconomy* and *#efficiencyeconomy* perspectives. People are being asked to do more and more, squeezing out every last drop of juice. But this is not sustainable because burning out is only a matter of time when you are treated like a machine.

We need to add a third dimension to the priority ranking: *relevance*. How much and for how long does this matter? Is it a momentary whim or a short-term benefit? Or is it something that will make tomorrow/the longer term better? From this, you can deduce the importance of the task and your role in making it happen. Here is a technique to address this issue:

- ♦ *H = Have to do it yourself*: failure to do so will significantly impact the long term.

- *I = It would be good to do it yourself:* missing a task will impact the long run. Do not do these tasks until the tasks in category P are done.

- *A = Automation solves the task*: the task is repetitive, has a clear structure, and is relevant in the long term. It can be automated in some way.

- *O = Others can do this, so move the task:* It matters in the long run, but I'm not the right person to do it.

- *N = Not worth wasting time:* all the remaining tasks fall into this category. So, these are left for last.

Naturally, you can add further subcategories, for example, with numbers for each level: *H1, H2, H3, and I1, I2, I3,* and so on. The important thing is not to move on to the I *category* tasks before the H *category* tasks have been solved (or are waiting for something to happen within a specific timeframe). The advantage of a lightweight task categorization like this is that it does not take much time to implement but adds significant value in all three dimensions: importance, urgency, and relevance. It allows you to use your time in the most efficient way overall, thus maximizing the effectiveness of your time use.

To put the above principle into practice, you can use the Concentration funnel below:

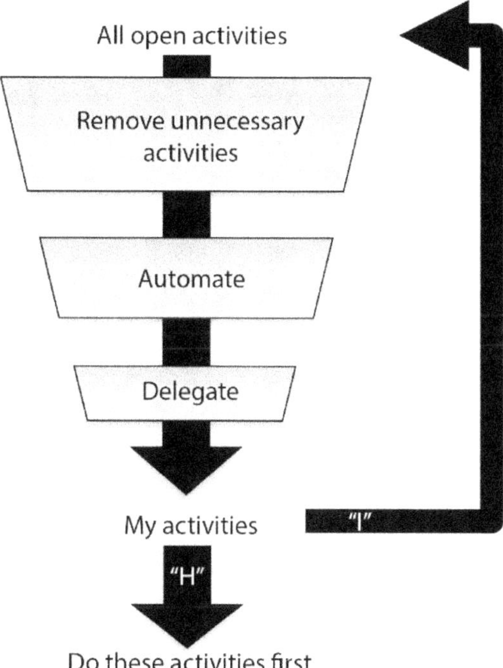

Put your tasks at the top of the funnel and run them through the *HIAON assessment*. Remove tasks that do not contribute to your long-term goals. Then, automate the tasks for which this is possible. Then delegate the tasks that you can to others. Now all you have left is a list of tasks that must be done, cannot be automated, and cannot be delegated to others. After that, you are left to decide whether the tasks are relevant: do they have to be done now (H), or can they be left for later (I)? They form your current to-do list if they must be done right now. Return them to the top of your Concentration funnel for later re-evaluation if they can be left for later.

This book has several sections on prioritizing things and using self-development to do the right things. And therein lies a secret to success: the more you do things that move you towards your goals, and the less time you waste on things that don't, the greater the likelihood of your success. The question then becomes not whether you will succeed but when it will happen. Don't be fooled by marketers' stories where someone became successful overnight; that's unlikely to be true (unless they won the lottery or some other luck-based game). In reality, they just did enough of the right things long enough to get over the threshold where success came to them.

Now that you know your to-do list, you can start implementing it daily. Below is an example you can use to plan your daily activities. I have used this template in my electronic diary for several years. In both Windows and macOS, it is possible to do automatic text hyphenation (for example, whenever you type the word *daily plan*, the operating system will replace the word with the background below).

The five most important things I want to achieve today:

1. Diary + 30 minutes of exercise + prayer

2.

3.

4.

5.

Hourly plan for the day (an illustrative example):

7:00   Morning activities, 30 minutes of exercise.

8:00   Daily planning and travel to work.

9:00   Work starts.

10:00   Small, healthy snack. Work.

11:00   Work.

12:00   Work.

13:00   Healthy, preferably vegetarian lunch. Work.

14:00   Work.

15:00   Work.

16:00   Small snack. Intense 5-10 minutes of gymnastics.

17:00   Work.

18:00   Travel home. Prepare dinner.

19:00   Dinner with the family. Relaxing.

20:00   Advancing objectives.

21:00   Advancing objectives.

22:00   Meditation, tomorrow's plan for the day.

23:00   Sleep

Today's main points:

♦ I will only focus on the things I can influence today.

♦

♦

I am grateful for these things today:

+

+

+

I learned these things today:

♦

♦

♦

The progress I made today:

+

+

+

Things that caused you stress, worry or grief:

-

The previous daily plan is an example that you can adapt to suit your needs. I recommend creating your base, which you can easily use every day and thus save time thinking about the content rather than writing it. Now that we have worked through prioritizing both tasks and our time, we can move on to the next topic: our habits, which guide everything we do, like the autopilot of an airplane.

What kind of habits do you have?

Science has shown many times that we humans are slaves to our habits. This may sound bad, but it can work against and for us. Good habits automatically lead us towards our goals, while bad habits make life difficult. If you are used to going for a run every day for half an hour, a good habit will prolong your life, increase your resistance, and boost your spirits. But if you're used to smoking cigarettes or snuff every day, you'll get the opposite effect. Both habits have their effects, and many things in life don't happen simultaneously because of thousands of small things. Very rarely will a few cigarettes directly cause lung cancer, or skipping a jog one day make you fat. But if it happens almost 300 days a year, that's 3,000 times in ten years, and so the problems (or benefits) have been building up through your habits over a long period of your life, and it's only a matter of time before their consequences catch up with you. And because this happens without us noticing, the incredible power of habits is hidden in our lives!

Achieving challenging goals is almost impossible in practice without adapting our habits to fit them or our current habits to support them in the future. For example, when I started running, I neither exercised nor jogged. My habits were poor concerning my goal of achieving the fitness level required for the *Navy Seals* entrance test. Those who know me from my past life would not have believed that I could achieve that fitness level as a hooked computer over-user on a moonlit day. So, I had to adopt new habits or change my goal. But something about reaching that fitness level tempted me to change my goals. And so, a couple of years later, I can't think of a day without a jog (unless I have a recovery day, which is also part of the sport). The same thinking applies to your life, and so you need to evaluate your habits and relate them to the goals you want to achieve.

If you want to go deeper into habit change, James Clear has written a book on *Atomic Habits*, which contains 300 pages more on the subject. However, I have applied his and my habit-forming experience to this book in a slightly more practical format. Of course, habit forming takes effort, but it is worth it. Our habits are so ingrained that we must consciously try to change them. Our habits revolve around a four-step circle that includes:

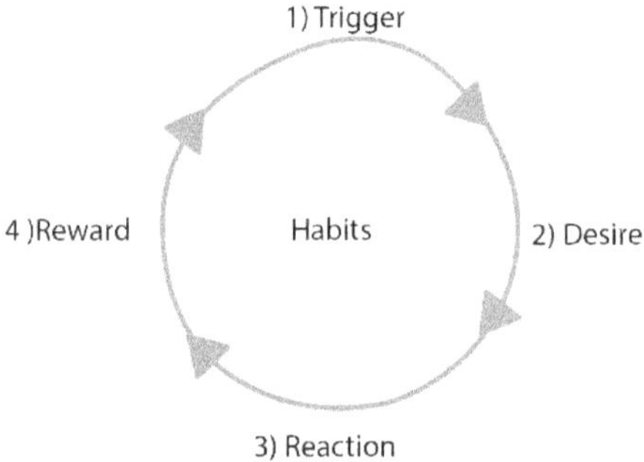

All our habits start with a trigger (1). It could be a thought, a sound, a smell, what you see, or something else. This trigger makes our brain want (2) something. The desire grows into a reaction (3), either satisfying the desire or ignoring it. And for this, we get the reward (4), i.e., the satisfaction of the desire in one form or another. Let's take a practical example from theory: you visit your friend who serves you a fresh donut, and you smell its wonderful aroma on the kitchen table. Naturally, you want to sink your teeth into that wheat and feel its warmth in your mouth, the taste on your tongue, and the smell on your nose. Every brain cell in your head is screaming to reach out for the treat, your jaws are already open, and drool is dripping from the tip of your tongue onto the tablecloth. If your brain has already got you to this point, you're unlikely to have the willpower to compliment your hostess and tell her that your goal is to drop a pound this month and leave the treat for another time. No, the fight is over, and another has reached your plate. So you've got your prize: a taste sensation and 300 kilocalories (and you'll need at least half an hour of brisk walking to burn off one of the donuts). But what if you had already changed your habits, and they automatically worked the other way? The story would now go differently. You visit a friend in the village, and he serves you a freshly baked donut. You smell its unique aroma on the kitchen table. Your brain tells you that this creation doesn't contain the nutrients you need, and you don't want to make the extra half-hour jog for it, so you're not interested in eating it either. So, you compliment your hostess on her fine baking and tell her that your goal is to drop a pound this month, so you'll save the treat for another time. That way, you'll be rewarded with more willpower and know you've done the right thing by both your hostess and you. Of course, she can still push it, and you can ask her to give it to you as a takeaway (and then throw it in the bin on the way). Everyone must look after themselves and others; that way, you can be polite to the hostess and save yourself the calories.

Straight to the heart?

What's the harm in having a donut to please the hostess? It is all too easy in life to overrate the big defining moments (when the hero of the story shoots the world's only special arrow into the heart of a dragon from a mile away without a scope) and underrate and ignore the small moments in life that are done daily (when the hero catches his 50th rabbit and roasts it on a campfire to eat to climb the mountain where the dragon lives for six months). Humans tend to imagine that great results require great one-off acts when the reality is quite the opposite. Often, great deeds are preceded by a vast number of small deeds. So, the result lies not in spectacular big deeds but in daily small ones. The difference between a hero and a loser is often that the *hero will work day after day towards one's goals, no matter how sexy it is*. This mindset applies no matter your goals (if you get straight to your primary goal, it might not have been so big). Achieving significant goals is very simple (not necessarily easy): you *only need to improve by 1% every day for a year to get a 37-fold improvement*. This is the so-called interest for interest phenomenon (which we also discuss in the economic chapter of this book). If you can walk 500 yards today, then walk 505 yards tomorrow, 510 yards the day after, 515 yards the third day, and so on. By the end of the year, you will be able to walk almost a half marathon!

Of course, the same works the other way around. If your activity declines by 1% daily, you're almost at zero by the end of the year. This is very easy to see with languages, for example. I once studied at Fudan University in Shanghai and could converse normally in Mandarin Chinese. However, I have not used a word of the language since 2007, and nowadays, I can hardly understand it and cannot hold conversations in Chinese. I'm sure you have similar experiences where old skills have rusted away with time. Both good and bad habits are crucial for us, as they are the interest rate for the development of ourselves. This is one of the most essential principles presented in this book. The more habits you have that support your goals, the more confident and sustainable you will be in achieving them. No habits are good or bad, but they all have consequences. It is entirely your choice whether you want to continue with habits that shorten or diminish the quality of your life. It is also your choice if you change your habits to support your life and your goals. No one should judge you for this. But make your choices in full awareness of them and act accordingly. If a cigarette pack every day is worth living at least ten years less and suffering more illness, then so be it. At least you know and acknowledge what you are doing. But remember that the effects of many unhelpful habits cannot be undone afterward.

The great challenge of personal habits is that it is sometimes difficult to see their impact. If you go to the gym every day, it's unlikely to show during the day because you'll come out with the same size biceps you went in with. But six months in the gym every day will show some. The same effect will be seen with indulging. You don't know that chocolate bar a day on the scale. But a bar a day for six months is visible on both the waist and the scale. You need to be aware of the impact of your small choices on significant effects. Even minimal changes in your habits can make a big difference to your life in the long run. You could even say that the impact is downright unfair. A small decision here and there has a significant effect. Our job is to bring this to our awareness and guide our actions. I use This thinking technique when it's raining outside, and a 20-mile jog awaits. If I skip the run, it won't affect me today, but it will affect my ultra marathon running program and thus potentially jeopardize my entire goal. So, I put on my raincoat and headed out the door, dreaming of an ultramarathon when I finished the run. On one of my runs, I forgot to bring a hat, and it started to hail on the way. Each piece of ice was like a pin prick in my forehead. I knew I could stop the run and return home (about half an hour earlier than the planned run). But I also realized that ultramarathons are not always run in good weather, and anything can happen in 60 miles. So, I put a smile on my face and shouted to the rakes: *come on, every sting in my face will help me run the ultra more confidently*. And so, I completed the planned run and got a lot of energy out of it. Thinking about this event in light of the steps that affect your habits is straightforward. The *trigger* was a hailstorm, the *desire* was to go home to warmth, the *reaction* was to turn the conditions into a training opportunity, and the *reward* was to beat another resistance on the way, which made me a stronger ultramarathoner. Had I returned home, the reaction would have been to give up, and the reward would have been the warmth of home prematurely. But the prize would have come at the possible expense of my dream, and I wasn't willing to sacrifice that. Success is a by-product of daily habits - not a one-off lottery win. Let's take more examples of how habits are the measure of our success (with a lag as noted earlier):

- ◆ Your financial success is a measure of your spending habits.

- ◆ Your weight is a measure of your eating habits.

- ◆ Your grades are a measure of how you study.

- ◆ Your skills are the measure of your training habits.

- The tidiness of your home is a measure of how organized you are.

- Your physical fitness is a measure of your exercise habits.

The list above should give you an idea of how the results of our lives relate to our habits. Although the daily, seemingly small things may seem insignificant, they still affect your results and your success in the long run. This also makes it challenging to adopt new habits because the work has to be done daily, and the results are only visible in the longer term.

You have gained new insights into our practices and their impact on our objectives. So now would be an excellent time to become aware of your habits. And there is a simple but effective exercise for that. We are not yet putting your habits together with your goals at this stage, but we are generally looking at them. Use the table below, with its three columns, to observe your daily habits for a week. In the first column, write down the habits that can have a positive impact on your life or the lives of others. In the middle column, write the habits that may be neither positive nor negative. In the last column, write the habits that may harm your life or the lives of others. This exercise aims not to change your habits but to become aware of them.

Positive habits	Neutral habits	Negative habits

Here is another illustrative example of using the table above:

Positive habits	Neutral habits	Negative habits
30 min jog	Reading the news	Nail biting
Brushing your teeth	Tending the garden	Nagging
Eating vegetables	Going to the bathroom	Review of others
Using dental floss	Weighing yourself	Looking at your phone first thing in the morning
Putting on deodorant	Turning off the Alarm clock	Farting

These are just examples, and you could have these same things in different columns, so you can put whatever daily habits you want in whichever column you want. The goal is to become aware of your habits. What does your list look like after a week?

If you already have clear goals, you can look at your list at this stage and tick off the habits you want to eliminate and those you want to strengthen. You can also think about which habits are missing from your list. It would be best to start doing them to be more confident of achieving your goals.

You can use the table below (or even your diary) to help you:

My goals are:

I want to strengthen my habits to help me achieve these goals.	My habits work against my goals, and I want to stop these.

Now that you know how your habits are helping, slowing, or even preventing you from achieving your goals, we can focus on increasing beneficial habits and eliminating unhelpful ones. We'll first go through an effective technique to help you do this.

You'll remember that habits go through a four-step cycle, from trigger to desire and fulfillment to reward. We need to develop ways to manage these four steps as easily and proactively as possible (if you want to be completely sober, it's easier if you're not buying a bottle of Coke from a liquor store). There is a process for creating and reinforcing good habits for each of the four steps:

1. Trigger: Make a good habit clear

2. Desire: Make a good habit desirable

3. Reaction: make a good habit easy

4. Reward: make a good habit of satisfying

Likewise, there is an antidote for eradicating bad habits at every stage:

1. Trigger: Make a lousy habit unnoticeable.

2. Desire: Make a lousy habit unpalatable.

3. Reaction: make a bad habit difficult.

4. Reward: make a bad habit unsatisfactory.

Now that you know what to do, you can easily ask at every stage what you need to do to make it happen. This will lead to a clear plan for each habit, whether reinforcing good habits or eliminating bad ones. We can do this with a simple list of things to help us. Let's start with the good habits first, using one imaginary good habit from a previous exercise as an example.

A good way: a 30-minute jog every day.

Make a good habit clear:

♦ I go for a 30-minute jog every day when I get home from work.

♦ When I walk in the front door, I immediately put on my jogging clothes.

Make a good habit desirable:

♦ I eat a delicious protein bar just before I go for a run. I only get a bar because I'm going for a run.

Make a good habit easy:

♦ I have more jogging clothes, so I always have a clean pair waiting at home when I come home from work.

> ◆ *My running shoes are waiting in the hallway, in the same place where I take off my work shoes.*
>
> ◆ *I have a raincoat in the hallway if it's terrible outside.*
>
> *Make a good habit satisfying:*
>
> ◆ *When I go for a run and arrive home, I drink a nice cup of relaxing Rooibos herbal tea and read the latest Donald Duck.*
>
> ◆ *I'm a runner and enjoy running, so a daily jog is part of my life.*
>
> ◆ *I get a star on my calendar for every run; I can go to dinner when I have 50 stars.*

Of course, the above are just examples; your list will look different. But hopefully, this will help you see how you can improve your good habits in concrete ways. So, what kind of things could you put on your list? Here are some tips to help you think:

Make a good way clear (trigger):

- Write down what your clear goals are in terms of habit. It would be best to be as specific as possible about what you do, when, and where you do it. For example, *I study Chinese every morning between 7:00 and 7:30 at the kitchen table.*

- Think about what triggers a good habit and how you can reinforce the trigger situation (for example, by getting into similar situations more often).

- Link good practices together, creating strong trigger chains. For example. This way, you generate chain triggers, where good habits trigger each other.

- Use tools to trigger good habits (e.g., stickers on the walls in the right places). Make the aids easy to spot.

Make a good habit desirable (desire):

- Chain together the things you must do and the things you want to do. For example, *I'll read the latest Donald Duck only after I've emptied the dishwasher.* Develop rewards for yourself for having a good habit.

- Take advantage of peer groups where reinforcing the same good habits comes naturally (for example, if you want to strengthen your prayer life, join a local church's prayer nights).

- Combine pleasure and challenging habits. For example, you could give yourself a protein bar before a run. This both fuels your run and healthily massages your taste buds. Of course, you won't eat a protein bar if you're not running.

Make a good habit easy (reaction):

- Remove all obstacles and obstacles to good practice. For example, if you want to stop drinking alcohol, don't keep it in your home.

- Keep everything you need for good manners easily accessible and on display. For example, if you want to eat healthily, keep fruit in plain sight in the kitchen and treats at the back of the cupboard.

- Recognize the importance of small decisions in achieving big things. Learn to master the moment of reaction.

- Keep good habits small enough so that they're not too much trouble to do.

- Make good habits as automatic as possible. Use technology, diary, calendar, etc. to help you. Give yourself reminders at essential places and times.

Make a good habit satisfying (reward):

- Find it rewarding and enjoyable to do the right thing.

- Give yourself an appropriate reward after a good performance.

- Keep track of your good habits and the number of habits you have, for example, by keeping a diary.

- If you miss one performance, don't miss another, but use the missed opportunity as motivation to be more accurate the very next time.

And here's a blank sheet to develop your good habits (you can also do this in your diary or on paper to evaluate all your good habits from the list you made earlier).

A good way:

Make a good way clear (trigger):

-
-
-

Make a good habit desirable (desire):

-
-
-

Make a good habit easy (reaction):

-
-

Make a good habit satisfying (reward):

Next, let's look at eliminating bad habits. In practice, you can take the opposite approach to eliminating bad habits compared to good ones. Let's take a practical example:

Bad habit: Biting nails

Make a lousy habit unnoticeable:

* *Keep gloves on.*

* *Keep hands in your pocket.*

Make a lousy habit unpalatable:

* *Get an expensive manicure that will make your nails beautiful.*

Make a lousy habit difficult:

* *Cut your nails short so that they are impossible to chew.*

Make a lousy habit unsatisfactory:

* *Give a friend $20 every time you bite your nails.*

Of course, the above are just examples; your list would look different this time, too. But this will help you see how to take concrete steps to eliminate your bad habits. So, what kind of things could you put on your list? Here are some tips to help you think about them:

Make a lousy habit unnoticeable (trigger):

- ♦ Reduce the opportunities to trigger the bad habit (e.g., avoid situations, people, places, etc. that trigger this terrible habit in you).

- ♦ Remove from your sight anything that triggers a bad habit (for example, if you want to lose weight, don't keep treats in sight).

Make a lousy habit unpalatable (desire):

- ♦ Change your mindset so that you see the reward of a bad habit as a negative thing you don't want to get (for example, eating a chocolate bar makes your stomach grow). The more aversive you make the reward of this bad habit in your mind, the less you will want to make this habit.

Make a lousy habit difficult (reaction):

- ♦ Make it as difficult as possible to make the bad habit. Increase the distance between you and the bad habit as much as possible. For example, if you want to stop using snuff, don't keep snuff available so you can go out and buy it when you feel like it. And once you've had one snus, throw the rest in the bin (which also makes it very expensive to use).

- ♦ Make an accountability pact with your friend (read more about it in this book) to get a stick whenever you make a bad habit.

Make a lousy habit unsatisfactory (reward):

- ♦ Ask others to point out to you if you do something terrible.

- ♦ Make it expensive and inconvenient for you to do the wrong thing. For example, automate money leaving your account every morning at 7 am if you sleep late. This way, if you don't wake up on time, you lose money because you didn't cancel the transfer.

And here's a blank sheet for you to use to cross off your bad habits (you can also do this in your diary or on a piece of paper so you can review all your bad habits from the list you made earlier).

A bad habit:

Make a lousy habit unnoticeable (trigger):

❖

❖

❖

Make a lousy habit unpalatable (desire):

❖

❖

❖

Make a lousy habit difficult (reaction):

❖

❖

❖

Make a lousy habit unsatisfactory (reward):

❖

❖

❖

Now, you know how to identify and develop ways to support your goals. The more you work on developing your habits, the more automatic they become, just like the previous habits. It's important to remember that people who make clear plans to build their habits are more likely to succeed. Many who think they lack the motivation to develop their habits need more clarity on how to do it concretely. These guidelines will help you make sure you're spending time on the right things to achieve your goals. Now that you're up to speed, the next step is to consider how to assess your progress.

Assess progress and development

The most dangerous word in the world is *later*. It seems so harmless... *"I'll do it later"* and *"I'll get back to you later."* The more you use a word to pursue your goals, the more aimless life becomes, even though it may seem like a perfectly valid word. However, it very soon turns into the word *never*. We put things off so long that we don't even remember having to do them. The goal disappears, and the results do not come. A big reason why we use that disgusting word is that we often must do something that scares us or requires significant effort. Staying in your comfort zone is... well, nice. However, progress only happens in the growth zone, where change is needed. The word *later* can take many different forms:

- I'll do it tomorrow (next week or month).

- I'm too young/old/poor to do this.

- Now is not the best time to promote this issue.

- As soon as I graduate from school, I can start.

- I'll do it when my kids are a bit older.

- I will start it on New Year's Eve.

- I need a bit more experience to do it.

- I'll start it when I'm retired / on holiday / somewhere else.

- I still need some money before I can start.

All of these are *later* manifestations of the word in our lives. I have been guilty of this kind of procrastination. It's just so tempting to do things later... That's why it pays to focus on starting where you are now. That's the best place and time to take the first step towards your goals. The opposite of *later* is *now*. You need to take a step towards your goals now, not later. And to do that, you need a big enough reason. Without internal motivation, it's hard to get yourself moving, so always think carefully about why you want to set specific goals because weak reasons to reach them won't get you there. Usually, the reason is either something fascinating or disgusting sufficient to want to avoid. Psychologically, it usually works better for people to prevent bad things than to get good things. Perhaps your goal supports both motivational styles, and you can switch between them depending on which one gets you moving better right now. Quitting smoking and snuffing are the most common goals I've seen dozens of people around me try and fail to achieve. They don't feel they have a strong enough reason to quit. For a friend of mine, however, it was different. His little girl brought a packet of cigarettes to her daddy and, pointed to the word *cancer on* the lid with her finger and said *Daddy, I don't want you to die because I love you.* He never had another cigarette from that moment on. Do you put knives in the dishwasher blade side up? In one family, a child under ten years old died when he tripped near an open dishwasher and ended up with a knife in his head. I have been putting knives in the dishwasher with the handle up since I heard about this incident. Sometimes, it is straightforward to find motivation when you give things a specific meaning.

In addition to strong motivation, another thing to squash delay is to do the essential things first. Often, people are advised to start with something easy and small (and of course, that's ok if it works for you), but in general, it's better to start with the most important things first, whether they're easy or hard, big or small. When you achieve things in order of importance, spend your energy first where it will have the most impact. And the more you get things done, the more you want to do them.

Third, divide the crucial tasks into appropriately sized chunks. There's an old saying that an elephant is eaten one piece at a time, so divide your tasks into appropriately sized chunks, say an hour, and accomplish them one at a time, many in a row. For example, if I think daily that *I need to get at least 61 100 words in this book,* despair quickly takes over. But if I think *I'm going to write today about avoiding procrastination because it's important for my readers and my own goals* before I know it, I've got a couple of thousand words on the topic. In the same way, you can keep track of how you're progressing most effectively and break down your tasks into sections that maximize progress.

The fourth important thing is recognizing that people cannot do many things simultaneously. They can only do one at a time, many in a queue. This leads to the critical conclusion that you remove all distractions around you. Don't put the TV on in the background. Don't scroll through social media while you're advancing your goals. I've found that music helps focus on what you're doing, but it needs to be music that doesn't have singing. So, I listen to electronic and classical music when concentrating on writing a book, working, or doing other tasks requiring concentration. What works for you?

Finally, we consider the importance of time. Many people like to talk about the past, but as the band sang: "Before was before, and now is now." Others like to dream about the future, but in reality, we only have one period: this moment. Carpe Diem - seize the moment is all we have. So, *how you use this very moment* is always the question.

The period under review plays an essential role in achieving and evaluating results. For 50 years, the American sociologist Edward Banfield (from Harvard University) studied the determinants of human success and positive economic progress in society. He identified one of the most critical factors as the ability to take a long-term view. This means being able to look beyond your current actions: *how does what I am doing/thinking right now affect my goals?* There is a big difference between achievers and losers regarding the time frame they feel about things. Successful ones take the long view and assess how what's going on in the moment affects it. Losers, on the other hand, only worry about the present and the immediate future. Successful people imagine the kind of person they want to be and the things they want to achieve over their lifetime, not just in the next exam or project. They also think in as much detail as possible about what they need to achieve to get there. It doesn't come without sacrifice because visualizing this kind of thing takes time. They want to make sensible choices between short-term pleasures and long-term goals. They will sacrifice the joy of the moment to get more significant results and rewards in the longer term. I learned this the hard way during my doctoral studies. It took me evenings and weekends for five years to get my degree because I worked full-time as a top-tier management consultant alongside school. It meant missing out on many student evening lectures, TV shows, and other momentarily satisfying things because of the goal. The mindset is not just about specific goals but about your entire lifestyle, from marriage, earning, and career advancement to any other aspect of life that is important to you.

Mistakes are an inevitable part of everyone's life. We cannot avoid our mistakes and those of others or the inconvenience of changing circumstances. So, it's no good trying to prevent mistakes too much, but it's better to think about your actions through risk management. We all remember how we felt as children when we did something wrong and our parents gave us some punishment for it. It was, helplessly, a dent in our self-esteem. Many of us are stuck in that emotional lock from childhood, which makes us feel inferior, low self-esteem, and shame when we make a mistake. For many, it feels better not to try too hard than to fail. However, such a mindset is not suited to our purposes, as something will go wrong sooner or later. And the challenge is not in avoiding mistakes but in dealing with them. One of my most significant life-changing insights was that mistakes are an opportunity to learn, not be punished. The voice in my head no longer says *you did wrong and are therefore bad*, but asks: *why did this result happen? What should I do differently next time*? When you take an objective view of your own and others' mistakes, even the emotions are relieved. There is no longer any reason to think badly of yourself (or others), and you can say, hey, I'm like Edison, *who found 1,000 different ways not to make a light bulb*. There will be one that works for you! The most common patterns of thinking that are detrimental to self-esteem and, therefore, to one's progress that I have encountered when coaching people are:

- *Martyrdom:* I am a victim of my own life or situations. Life happens to me more than I happen to live because other people, luck, fate, or even God determine what happens to me, and therefore, I am not entirely responsible for my life*. It is straightforward to fall back on this thinking when life is going through major upheavals.

- *Inner critic:* my value is determined by what I do and what I have. I am not enough and worthless because I did not perform well enough. I punish myself and others when things go differently than planned.

- *Low ambition:* life's busyness and urgencies determine what I focus on. I don't think about the bigger picture and am willing to put off momentary pleasure for bigger goals.

- *Talk without action:* I talk about things until they become true. And I talk and dream about doing things without doing enough to make them happen.

- *Creating the future from the past:* I can't do things because I haven't done them before. Or I failed at something in the past, so I can't try again.

Another critical insight to help you assess your development is putting aside your feelings of unworthiness and comparing yourself only to yourself, not others. If you start comparing yourself to the best in the

---

* God does have good plans for you, but it's up to you to follow them. Jer. 29:11. *My thoughts are of peace, and not of destruction: I will give you a future and a hope."*

world, your goal may feel unattainable. There are so many people in this world that even if you are the best in the world for one moment, it won't last long. Soon, someone else will come along and do it even better (think of how sports records are constantly being broken, for example). So, it's healthier to understand where you are and where you want to be and focus on the tasks and thoughts that will lead you toward that goal. When you change your thinking this way, the feeling of worthlessness becomes worthless. What does it matter what others do and are because you are striving to be your best self? One of the best advice I have received from my Christian mentor, John C. Maxwell, is not to compare yourself to others. And that has helped. There is a place for each of us in this world, just as we are, so there is no point in running after other people's desires, and it is better to focus on our own. Accept personal responsibility for yourself and your results; you will have a sound basis for evaluating your progress against your goals. By now, you will have realized that your development is about getting closer to your goal and growing as a person. It is essential for a healthy self-esteem to be aware of the following:

- I am valuable because of who I am, not what I do or own.

- I am fully responsible for my life. I can choose, if not the situation, how I react and respond.

- I learn from the past but don't live in it. I will keep the lessons and let everything else go.

- I focus on the most essential things, thinking about how each moment and each thing contributes to my long-term goals. Focusing on the right things is extremely important in my life.

- I understand that if I don't achieve what I want in life, I must change how I think about the things that affect it.

An easy way to ensure that you maximize your focus on the right things is to narrow the time frame in which you look at things and ask what you can do to improve them. If you see grandma slipping on the street and breaking her arm, you are unlikely to start thinking about her future and whether she can spoon her morning porridge into her mouth. More likely, you'll take her to the hospital for treatment. However, when something goes wrong in our lives, we often focus on looking for blame in the past and thinking about the consequences of what happened. It is best to focus on stopping the problem from continuing, preventing it from happening again, and moving on to the new situation that the situation has caused in the best way possible.

Liability Agreement

Sticking to your goals can sometimes be difficult, especially when challenging. Things happen in life (such as the coronavirus, forced redundancy, job changes, and family changes) that can easily make anyone give up on their goals and focus on other things. If your goals are essential, such factors should not stop you. One effective way to combine optimizing progress, assessing progress, and self-development together is to use what is known as an accountability contract with a friend. This is a contract you make yourself based on your goals and where you define what will happen if you don't reach your goals. You then seal the deal with your buddy, to whom you are accountable for the goals and the consequences of not reaching them.

The accountability contract (called Acco among friends) aims to make not reaching targets even more painful than reaching them. Let's say you want to lose a pound a month for six months. Acco might say that every month you fail to drop a kilo (you'll be weighed to prove the result), you give your mate $500. That way, you go to the weigh-in once a month with five hundred in hand, and one of you comes out of there with a big smile on their face. Of course, your carrot and stick can be whatever you want, but the stick has to be bigger than the carrot. Otherwise, it won't be enough to motivate you in difficult moments (for example, if you only had to give your friend $10, it wouldn't bother you much if you missed that month's pound). When the threat is real, it helps you stay focused on achieving your goals. If you don't do enough in one month, you'll remember it the next. So, you need to assess your progress regularly while motivating yourself with a stick (not just a carrot). The Acco approach works on many aspects of our lives. For example, bills have a due date and a late payment fee, aiming to ensure that the biller receives the money within the agreed time. Similarly, a gym has a monthly fee wasted if you don't go to the gym (they don't give you a refund at the end of the month if you don't use the service). People are generally so bad at keeping track of their goals that one Danish gym chain decided to cash in. Customers make a deal with them that if they go to the gym at least twice a week, every week of the month, they don't have to pay anything. But if they miss one session, they pay the average gym fee. The business thrives because many people join thinking they will get a free gym membership, but most, after the initial excitement wears off, end up paying for it in vain.

What should Acco be like, then? It's up to you what you want to put in there, but a good Acco includes:

- Between whom is the contract made (i.e., you and your accountability buddy)?

- What is your goal, and for how long?

- What happens if you don't reach your goals?

- How will the target be monitored, and how often will it be measured/checked?

- Signatures, place, and date.

Acco resembles a typical contract, where two parties agree on certain things. Of course, this agreement is one-sided because your friend is not directly responsible for anything, but you are. Your friend is just supporting you in the process. Here is a ready-made basis for you to use:

Liability Agreement

Responsible person:_______________________________

Accountability partner: _______________________________

The responsible person will do everything possible to reach
the following targets and timetable:

If the responsible person fails to achieve these goals, the
consequences will follow:

And this will be followed up:

Signatures

Signature of the responsible person:

____

Signature of the accountability partner:

Place and time: ______________________

You can use the base above directly or modify it to suit your needs. Let's go through an example:

Example of a responsibility agreement

Responsible: *Will Smith*
Accountability partner: *Peter Johnson*

The responsible one will do everything possible to reach the following targets and timetable:

Will aims to lose one pound of weight monthly for six months. His starting weight today is 213 pounds as of 14.5.2024 on the Garmin Index scale. The goal is to lose weight as follows:

by 14.6.2024, 210 pounds
by 14.8.2024, 200 pounds
by 14.10.2024, 190 pounds

Will's target weight in 6 months is 170 pounds or less.

If the person responsible does not reach these targets, the consequence is that every month Will does not reach the above target, Will will give Peter 100 $. Will will come to the weighing with Peter in the above schedule with 100 $. The money is put on the kitchen table to wait for the weighing. If Will is on target, he gets to keep the $100. If Will is not at his target weight, Peter gets to keep $100.

This is monitored by weighing the Garmin Index on the scales once a month, on the 14th of the month, for the next six months.

Signatures

This example contract makes Will responsible to Peter for six months, and Peter can get rich from this experience between $0 and $600, depending on how hard Will works to reach the target. The first month is still relatively easy for Will because, in the worst case, Will can go to the toilet on a "big deal" before the weigh-in and not eat or drink on the day of the weigh-in, wear light clothes or be naughty, and he will probably lose a pound. But by the second month, it would have been quite a trip to the toilet if that was his plan of action, and by the third month at the latest, Peter would have gained his $100 if Will wasn't serious about the target. And, of course, it is good to remember that in the end, Will can only fool himself because it is not Peter but Will and the carrot and stick he has set up.

 Now, you have the necessary evidence to monitor your progress and development, and you can fire away toward the goal while enjoying the journey.

Go back towards the goal and enjoy the journey

The outcome of your efforts depends on both the actions and circumstances. Sure, we do our best to control events, but chaos is part of life and the world, and we often encounter unexpected events (something breaks, someone dies, a viral pandemic strikes, you win the lottery, etc.). Viktor E. Frankl, if anyone, has made it clear from his concentration camp experiences that while we cannot always choose the circumstances of our lives, we can always choose how we react and respond to them. Any outcome is the consequence of an event and the effect of our reaction to it. This is a relatively small but potent tool for life management: *choose your response regardless of the event and ensure the best possible outcome regardless of the circumstances.* Although Viktor E. Frankl was a genuine victim in a German concentration camp, he chose survival over sacrifice. Much has been written about responsibility in this book. While we are not always responsible for what happens to us, we are always personally responsible for how we deal with it.

Goethe said that *everything is difficult before it is easy*. This is especially true when it comes to changing your habits. Bad habits are usually effortless to adopt but challenging to live with long-term. Good habits, on the other hand, are often more challenging to adopt, but they are pleasant to live with. I'm sure you know this from your own experience. What good habits do you have that were once difficult to adopt but are now suitable for your quality of life? For myself, I can mention exercise. I used to have not the slightest interest in exercise, and as a result, I not only had poor fitness but also a sore back, fatigue, lack of energy, and inactivity. Since starting regular, adequate exercise, my energy levels have increased, and I have beaten myself many times over in physically and mentally challenging goals. But this has not come without pain and mistakes. The old me cried out loudly to return to the couch with Netflix instead of a jog. So, it's essential first to decide and describe your new desired habit and then list your reasons for wanting it. Then, you must start forming the habit through self-development and give grace when slips occur. And when they do, you need to think about why the slip happened and what you can do next time to prevent it before it happens. In this way, the good new habit can be reinforced step by step until it becomes automatic and no longer requires conscious watching and reinforcement—this kind of progress towards your goals almost by itself.

What is the difference between a hero and a coward?

We have fears and uncertainties about ourselves and our actions, which is normal. The difference in results is due to how you deal with those fears, primarily because surpassing yourself requires going into a growth zone. So, what is the difference between a coward and a brave person? A Brave person uses their self-development skills to face and overcome their fears. On the other hand, cowards let their fears take over and submit to them. The old saying goes that *in war, the difference between a hero and a coward is that the hero stays on the battlefield for five minutes longer.* Fears also affect what we fear will happen. Someone afraid of blushing at speeches will make himself blush more and more because of fear. Fortunately, this can also be reversed, and you can make it your business to blush when you go to speak. This reverse psychology removes the fear, and the fearful person no longer blushes. The skill of dealing with fear has had a significant impact on my own life, and it didn't come to me painlessly. The most significant change began when I was in northern Finland in the early 2000s, hosting an event with over a thousand people in the audience. One of my tasks was to introduce a well-known Finnish actress who came on stage next to give a lecture on positivity. After I had introduced her and she came out from behind the curtain, the actress took the microphone from my hand, thanked me for the beautiful introduction, and kissed me on the stage right on the mouth. The audience applauded; I went behind the curtain, and this lady started her lecture (and used me as an example). Almost 20 years later, just writing about this still gives me a rush of emotion. Am I now embarrassed for the rest of my life? What did his kiss mean? Did he want something more (despite the 40-year age difference)? Will I still be able to work as a presenter after this? I wondered what the thousands who saw this would think of me. Fear gripped me until I was shaking in the back room. Worst of all, I knew I would have to go back on stage to thank the speaker and introduce the other speakers who were still to come. I managed to calm down during the lecture and composed myself enough to finish my work, but my hands were still shaking for the rest of the day. It also didn't help that I tried to make a half-hearted joke about the event in my closing summary, and it didn't entertain the audience either with laughter or applause. The rest of the day was a total disaster because I lived through it with fear. It was only much later that I realized what had happened that day as I went over it in my head repeatedly. I could not deny that fear had paralyzed me. So, I developed a list for myself that I could quickly go through in my mind to overcome my fears:

- Is this a life-threatening situation for you or others? If not, go ahead; if yes, how can I save lives?

- Is this a threat to your health or the health of others? If not, go ahead; if yes, what can I do to avoid accidents?

- Could this cause you or others significant harm? If not, go ahead; if yes, how can I reduce the risk?

With this list, I have survived many situations where fear could have paralyzed me easily (and stopped many of the people I was with from doing something great, like skydiving). By following the principles outlined in this book, I have overcome both my fear of heights and my fear of deep water to the point where I skydive and am a certified PADI diving instructor. I achieved both goals as part of my ambition to overcome my fear. Perhaps the fears were very deeply embedded in me, as I still don't go either out the door of an airplane or off the back of a boat into the water without a quick mental review to ensure that I have maximized the risk management of the situation based on the above issues. I think I got a fear of heights as a child when I fell off the roof of a building and most of my teeth were left on the landing site (the bloodstain left on my clothes as I walked back home is still fresh in my mind especially since I had to use multiple braces afterward to straighten out the teeth). My fear of deep water probably came from the fact that we used to have a swimming pool at home with bubble wrap on top to keep the water warm. Once, I got the brilliant idea of going under the edge and coming up from the middle. I didn't realize that once the plastic is stuck in the water, it doesn't come off because it doesn't get replacement air from anywhere. So, I almost drowned when, with empty lungs, I first tried to get the plastic wrap up and then dived back to the edge with my last breath. But instead of fear stopping me from doing these things, it has become an asset for me, making sure I'm awake and sharp when needed. The past fear is my current courage. Of course, I have other fears that I have had to overcome, such as my father's business bankruptcy in the 1990s and the resulting fear of financial failure. It took me a long time to learn that money comes and goes, but my security is in God, not money*. It has not only removed the fear of the economy but has also laid a healthy foundation for a whole life where money is just a tool. We learn from all that life brings and let go of the goal. And we also know that despite setbacks, we will enjoy the journey because what doesn't kill us strengthens us!

Straighten the corners and move forward with courage!

The road is full of bends when we let go of the goal. So, effective problem-solving techniques are an essential part of achieving challenging goals. Problems can be solved in many ways, and your personality will influence how you solve them. So, the only way to learn problem-solving skills properly is to put yourself in situations where you must solve them.

Here's a powerful 10-step approach to problem-solving that you can use as a basis for developing your skills (another skill that none of us will ever fully master):

1. Stop and calm down. In panic mode, you're just going to get sloppy. How big is this problem on a scale of 0 to 10, where at level 0, the problem is irrelevant, and at level 10, someone could die?

2. Define the problem as precisely as possible. The better you know the problem, the more effectively you can solve it.

3. Check that the problem is a problem that needs a solution. Not all situations are worth solving. How important will it be to solve this problem in six months?

---

* "... I have learned to make do with what I have. I know poverty and prosperity, I am used to everything and anything, to eating my fill and going hungry, to living in abundance and scarcity. I can bear it all with the help of him who gives me strength." Philippians 4:12-13

4. Look beyond the problem. What other related issues might be problems? And how are these problems related, if at all?

5. Find the root cause of the problem. What led to this problem? Was this a one-off event, or is this a recurring problem? What triggers this problem?

6. List all the possible solutions you can come up with. The more alternative ways you come up with to solve the situation, the more likely you are to find the best option. Avoid single-solution situations, as experience has shown that the quality of the final solution is related to the number of solution options considered.

7. Choose the best solution options. Sometimes, any solution is better than none, so what are the best options for these solutions, and which ones can you leave out?

8. Decide and choose the most appropriate solution in this situation. Evaluate whether the solution you have chosen is effective in this situation.

9. Hold yourself and others involved in the solution accountable to make it happen—set metrics to show that the solution has been implemented and the outcome sought has been delivered.

10. Run a solution to the problem.

Some say that guts can get you through any problem or situation. Here's a test to help you assess your ability to stay on your chosen path and enjoy it, whatever the circumstances. All questions are on the same scale. Choose one option for each question. Once you have answered these, we can then calculate what we call your "True Grit Factor"[*] and what you can do with it:

---

[*] This test is adapted from a scientific article by Duckworth, Peterson, Matthews & Kelly (2007) to fit the purpose of this book.

True Grit test

For Part A questions, put your answers in numerical order as follows:

5 = Describes me very well
4 = Describes me well
3 = Sounds a bit like me
2 = Does not describe me well
1 = Does not describe me at all

I have overcome significant challenges and achieved essential goals

I am not easily discouraged by setbacks

I am hardworking

I finish what I start

I have achieved a goal that took me years to achieve

I am careful

I have ways to grow outside my comfort zone

For Part B questions, put your answers in numerical form as follows:

1 = Describes me very well
2 = Describes me well
3 = Sounds a bit like me
4 = Does not describe me well
5 = Does not describe me at all

New ideas and projects sometimes take me off track from my current goals

My interests vary from year to year

I have been very interested in some ideas and projects but lost interest later.

I set myself targets, but I change them often

I find it challenging to stay motivated for tasks that take six months or more

I start new projects, hobbies, or things in my life every few months

I have a very short temper, so I lose my nerve quickly

Calculating the factor of contents

Now add up all the numbers and write down the total:

Now divide this number by 14 (i.e., the sum of the scores / 14) and round to one decimal place.

My True Grit Factor is:

Your True Grit Factor can be any number between 1 and 5. If your True Grit Factor is less than 3.5, you should consider how to raise your True Grit Factor. If you score 4 or above, you are in a good place in your True Grit Factor and, therefore, more likely to achieve your goals. Of course, you can continually improve, so I recommend you take a moment to reflect and write down below in which areas and how you could increase your level of Grit.

This is how I can grow my guts:

Help, my hourglass is draining fast...

At this stage, when you're letting go and enjoying the journey, it's easy to run into time management challenges. We've covered this topic before, but as it's very likely that you're either in a full-time day job or studying, it significantly impacts time management. For my part, I have found that, especially at this stage when you are pursuing your dreams and goals, day jobs can easily take up most of your time and thus slow you down. What factors can help you perform well at work or school and free up time for your goals?

- Work as much as your contract requires; working overtime will not benefit you in terms of your other objectives. If it is impossible to do your work within the agreed time, negotiate with your employer to make your workload realistic. A standard working week is 40 and 8 hours a day, five days a week, so aim for that. Also, don't spend extra time at work, even with free beer and a games room, because you can use this time to develop yourself and focus on your more important goals.

- Identify and manage expectations of you in the workplace. It's better to do three things well at work than 30 things mediocre. If you do your core tasks well, the perception of your performance by others will not go down, even if you don't work long hours or overtime (see previous point).

- Related to the previous point, don't create or agree to absurd timetables. Overly tight and unrealistic schedules are like timewasters, causing stress and increasing inefficiency. It's okay to have schedules, but they should be reasonable and not change. If you must be ready by Friday of next week, you must be prepared by Friday. But what can and should change as necessary is the workload of the schedule. And this, too, can only become less, not more. So, schedules must not be inflated by additional work or stretched by falling behind.

- Tick off the extra tasks. Read fewer newsletters and blogs. Don't do other people's work that you shouldn't be doing. Read and send fewer emails. Attend fewer meetings and phone calls and insist on a precise schedule and goal.

- Work on your own time rather than in real-time. Don't immediately jump at every request and command, but prioritize your tasks. If you are asked for a lot of advice, set up office hours when available. This will protect your working time and make it more efficient.

- Do your work as independently as possible and reduce your dependence on others. That way, you get things done faster and don't waste time waiting for others to do things or correcting what they've done.

- Favor and develop policies, rules, and practices that work in the long term. Improve the process rather than individual tasks. This will ensure that you deliver value more sustainably.

- Don't get lost in the world of struggle. More work does not mean more results. The more you work, the less effective and creative you become. Today's glorification of toil is unhealthy and, therefore, not for you because burnout will put you on the dock, not make you more effective.

- Set aside an appropriate amount (for example, 20%) of working time for essential but unscheduled tasks (such as activities or self-development). Don't waste all your time responding to messages and issues.

- Keep your plan flexible so you can easily switch to the tasks that matter most now. Don't lock things in too far into the future so you can respond to changing situations and needs.

Don't put yourself in a situation where you must do something that is not the best use of your time at that moment. And if you're already doing the wrong thing, rudely interrupt and acknowledge the situation. There's no point in continuing to waste time in that situation.

- Divide your work into 60-minute periods, with a 5–10-minute break to move around and change scenery. This will ensure that your efficiency stays up throughout the hour. Fragmented working hours are more stressful and reduce your concentration.

- Don't allow interruptions, as they cut off your thoughts and reduce your effectiveness. Whenever you must change the subject in your head (for example, from cars to carrots), your brain has first to store the current situation (what you thought about cars), find out what you know about the new subject (carrots), and then download this new information for you to use. Sure, this happens quickly, but it interrupts your thought process badly. So, don't allow your colleagues or others to interrupt you while you're focused on doing something. If you are in a role where others need to ask you for help, then set up office hours (you can, for example, include them in the email signature) when you are available for questions. For instance, you could open an hour in the morning and an hour in the afternoon for questions but not be available at other times.

- Set aside time in your calendar to do work, and don't keep an open calendar where anyone can book time whenever they want. Your time is your most important resource, so protect it accordingly.

- Keep real-time communication tools, such as online chats, telephone, etc., muted or switched off when working in a focused way. These cause interruptions in your thought process and slow you down. You can keep your communication tools on when you have set aside time.

- The option of doing nothing at all about certain things is often even the best. It should always be one of the options to consider. It is often easier to ruin things than to improve them, so it is worth evaluating rather than making a change for its own sake (there is no point in fixing what is intact). Also, consider the chain reactions caused by changes (buying new shoes leads to purchasing new socks leads to buying new trousers, etc.).

- Keep the size of your work teams appropriate. Often, a team of three will work. Two will have differences of opinion, four will need a fifth to make decisions because of tie votes, and a team of five or more is already difficult to manage. So, it's best to work in teams of three if possible.

- Learn to say no to things. It is indeed easier to say *no* than *yes*. And you don't have to say no to everything, but to certain things that don't contribute to your goals. And if you say *yes, make* sure that everyone involved understands exactly what you are saying yes to (because interpretations of what you commit will very quickly differ). *No* is a problematic word that helps you focus on the right things, whereas *yes* is an easy word but causes more stress and effort.

The list above will help you optimize your work or study efficiency so that you don't miss anything and free up your time to pursue other important goals. And, of course, many of the principles above will work to support you in your goal-focused tasks. At this stage of the "TO HUNDRED" process, you will focus on creating results as best as possible until you get there.

Reset and move on to new adventures

All of us are looking for happiness and success in our lives in one form or another. I doubt that many of us want to excel, set challenging goals, and race to meet them to feel bad or suffer. Indeed, there is often a gap in people's happiness between where they are now and where they want to be. An old saying illustrates this well: *success is about getting what you want, and happiness is about wanting what you get.* For very few people, having a lot of money, worldly possessions, fame, and glory brings true happiness[*]. Some people have nothing and are extremely happy, while others have everything, and even that is not enough. In recent years, Finland has been featured in many newspaper articles among the world's happiest countries[†]. Perhaps we, too, have learned something from this. Some do not see happiness as the primary goal or result but instead as a by-product of doing the right things. *For* me, at least, the thought that you, inspired by this book (or any other source), have the energy to realize yourself as the best you can be brings immense joy. **Enthusiasm brings enthusiasm. Happiness breeds happiness. It is not a finite resource or taken away from others.** So, when you reach your goals, it's good to pause to reflect on how you got here. Compare yourself to where you started and how you have progressed. What baseline tests did you do, and what results are you getting from them now? Perhaps the actual outcome doesn't matter much because the journey has been fun, and the thought of doing and achieving interesting new things gives you the enthusiasm to keep going. Finding meaning in life gives you happiness and the energy to do more, so where will your next adventure take you?

A reset doesn't necessarily mean quitting, but rather an intermediate stage where you reassess your progress and direction and think about where you want to go. *Self-development should never end!* And it doesn't matter if you reach the goals you set; it matters that you can say you tried your best and improved along the way. I don't always reach my goals either (*for example, I'm still far from my 200-push-up goal*), but that's not bad because

---

[*] For example, consider how life ended for Michael Jackson.
[†] https://www.stat.fi/tup/satavuotias-suomi/suomi-maailman-karjessa.html

I made progress in the process (*I'm already over 100*). We should always have a goal that is not so unrealistic that we can never get there, but that is so challenging that it is almost like a carrot on a stick for a donkey. It keeps us moving forward. Along the way, we must stop and assess how we're doing. That way, you can improve your effectiveness from different angles:

- *Improved productivity:* the earlier you can fix what you do and how you do it, the more you get done at the same time and with the same resources. In this book, we have discussed the importance of time and return on investment. Maximizing it is easier when you evaluate what you do often enough and objectively.

- *Growing talent:* The better you understand your talent, the better you can use and develop it. Many of us have resources that we don't always even realize we have because we don't take *stock of* our abilities often enough.

- *Better quality:* the earlier you find and correct bad habits, mindsets, action plan steps, and the like, the better you will get there. The quality of what you do makes a big difference, both in the result and along the way. Then you don't need to say: *A, you've got a hole in your head.*

- *More capacity:* the faster you get things done, the more you can do. Increasing your capacity allows you to use your time more efficiently. Regularly evaluating your performance helps you increase your capacity by eliminating unnecessary tasks and increasing the speed at which you complete essential tasks.

Let's get rid of the old things.

You can assess your performance in four steps that make up the acronym **PCMD**, taking the letters in order:

1.   Prepare.

2. Collect data.

3. Draw conclusions.

4. Decide what you do.

In this last step of the "TO HUNDRED" process, we want to prepare ourselves for the following challenges. You may have noticed that there were several self-assessment techniques in the book. These have been designed to help you get to know yourself better and, most importantly, identify areas of improvement that can enhance the quality of life for yourself and those around you. You can now go back to these tests, do them again, and compare your progress (assuming you read this book and did something about it). Let's go through the PCDD again, step by step.

The first P-step prepares the ground for the termination of the objective in question and an appropriate evaluation of what has been done to achieve it. So, what dreams did you achieve in the last six months? It isn't easy to monitor your progress if you do not decide which areas you want to improve. Then, turn your wishes into reality through action plans and action. SMART objectives help you to see where you are and how you have progressed along the way. So, prepare for a reset by looking back at what you set out to achieve.

The second C-step collects information that you can use to assess your situation. What tests do you need to retake to see your progress? What indicators did you set using SMART? What was your starting situation, and what is your current performance level? Bring all the information together. Depending on your goals and timetable, this should be done every few months to boost your self-esteem by seeing your progress in concrete terms. You can also think about the following questions to help you gather information on your progress:

♦ What things did you deliberately leave undone?

♦ What things wasted your time?

- What things could you have done better?

- Who helped you most to achieve your goals?

- Who was the biggest obstacle to achieving your goals?

- When did you let fear stop or slow you down?

- When were you courageous?

- What kind of things did you find particularly dull to do?

- What kind of things were particularly inspiring or motivating?

- What new good habits did you form?

- Which bad habits did you get rid of or reduce to a significant level?

The questions above will help you gather information and get to know yourself better. You can use the information you collect in the next step to draw further conclusions.

The third D-step concludes the information gathered so far. Go beyond the information you have collected and draw conclusions about what you will do more of and what you will do less of in the future. You can also use these evaluation questions:

- What did you learn from this process?

- What are you most proud of in the last six months?

- What reusable skills have you learned?

- If a journalist were to write about what you have achieved in the last six months, what would the article's title be?

- If you were to do this again, what would you do differently this time?

- What new things did you learn about yourself?

The more you can draw on your strengths and interests, the more effective you will become. When I think about my following goals (or reassess my current ones), I focus on five key areas:

- *Health and well-being:* How can I promote my physical and mental fitness?

- *Relationships:* How can I develop as a person for others and add even more value to them?

- *Productive work:* How can I optimize both my well-being and productivity at work?

- *Financial independence:* How can I free myself from the economic shackles to spend my time as it is best?

- *Self-development:* How can I become the best possible version of myself?

These questions are worth pondering. Did the goals you focused on over the last six months bring you closer to who you want to be?

In the final, fourth D-step, go back to your annual plan and update it. You can also make a new action plan for your next target. Reflect:

- What dreams do you still want to pursue in the future?

- What kind of things will you do more of in the future?

- What kind of things are you going to do less of?

- What good new habits do you want to form?

- Which bad habits do you want to get rid of?

These four steps will help you reset your current goals and move towards more meaningful new ones. This book is accompanied by some sample programs to help you get fit or even write a book. Plenty of ready-made self-development programs are available online, so you don't always have to reinvent the wheel. The main thing is to do things that move you and your life forward and increase your happiness and accomplishment.

Perhaps at this point, once you've achieved your six-month dream, you can return to your Top 5 list, do the exercise again, and start working towards your following goals. By now, you will also have learned how much time you can spend and what works for you in your self-development. In the next part of the book, we'll go over more scheduling issues to help you structure and schedule what you're doing. Good luck with your new adventures!

Part 3. IN SIX MONTHS

M It takes time to achieve relevant objectives. You have already made some initial timetable plans in the *Plan Your Way to Success* chapter, and you can use them as a basis for more detailed planning. The timescales you need will depend on several factors, including:

- The challenge of your goals.

- About the time you have available.

- The amount of work needed.

- On the resources available.

- Changes in circumstances.

- Your motivation and your ability to cope.

The adage warns that *no plan can survive first contact with the enemy*[*]. So please don't set your plans in stone but design them so that they can adapt to change as needed without too much trouble. The six-month timeframe chosen for this book is because it is difficult to achieve meaningful goals in less time, and longer may feel too far away. However, you can select a timeframe that feels right for you about the available time and the demands of the goal. As this book is a strategy guide, the advice on timing will also work whatever your objectives. The method presented here allows you to tailor the analysis's time and scope to suit your needs. The timetable is divided into four different sections:

---

[*] Count Helmuth von Moltke the Elder in the late 19th century.

- *Six months:* the main objective and sub-objectives are defined and prioritized at the top level.

- *Two months:* sub-objectives defined and prioritized.

- *Four weeks:* sub-objectives and their tasks defined and prioritized. Complete the tasks after the tasks below are completed. If necessary, you can move tasks from two to four weeks.

- *Two weeks:* tasks in a well-defined order and the form of completed tasks. Focus solely on completing these tasks.

You can shape the above timelines to suit your needs, but I recommend keeping in mind that the closer to implementation the tasks and objectives are, the more precisely they are defined and organized. The idea is to learn from your own doing and progress so that the goals and tasks ahead can change to ensure the best possible progress.

> *"They say that time changes things, but you have to change them yourself."*
> *- Andy Warhol*

Regardless of the timeframe, writing your objectives in both SMART and story format is advisable. This way, you describe what you want to achieve and do it in a format that is easy to understand and follow. Stories get your brain working more actively than just a few words, so you can write stories as descriptive as you like. At the top, six-month level, you may not need to add as much detail, as it can change as you progress. So, what is your main goal, and what are the related SMART sub-goals? Write them below:

My main objective is:

Sub-goals that will take me to my main goal within the next six months:

Now, you have a list of your main objectives and the main sub-objectives related to them. If possible, you can put them in order of importance. As you move closer to the tasks to be carried out, always focus on the most critical objectives first. Next, you can select the ones you think you can achieve in the next two months.

The sub-goals that will take me towards my main goal over the next two months:

Now, you have a more explicit list of goals to focus on over the next two months. The rest can wait their turn on the six-month list. But you'll update your lists every 2-4 weeks, so their time will come. Now that you know your goals for the two months, you can write down all the tasks involved in achieving them based on your action plan. For each goal, think about what you need to do to meet the goal. Please write down the list and prioritize it as best you can.

> *Activities that will take me towards my goals within the next four weeks:*

This will take you to the final stage, where you choose from the above tasks you can complete in the next two weeks. This will give you a list to focus your laser on for the next couple of weeks. The other tasks will wait their turn on the four-week list. Naturally, you may not know precisely how long each task will take. So, you can move tasks to the four-week list if there are too many or move tasks to the two-week list if there are not enough. This will ensure you always have the correct tasks to complete. And because you constantly update your lists as needed (at least every two weeks), you'll also have an overview of your progress and the goals and tasks required to achieve them. Research shows that it takes at least three weeks to form a new habit, so I recommend following this approach for at least the first month. You can then start to adapt it to suit you.

Daily calendar

Now that you have a timetabled action plan, you can print out a daily calendar on your wall to mark the days when you will progress towards your goals. Depending on your plan, you may have a tick mark for each day, but any good plan will also include some flexibility for days you miss. You can make your daily calendar or use the template below:

Daily calendar	Mon	Tue	Wed	Thu	Fri	Sat	Sun
Week 1.							
Week 2.							
Week 3.							
Week 4.							

The above scheduling example is just one way to implement your action plan. You can modify it as needed to suit your needs. The aim is to start with the main objective and work from there to individual tasks in a timetable, following specific steps:

- Define the main objective.
- Divide the main objective into sub-objectives of appropriate size.
- Prioritize the sub-objectives.
- Schedule sub-objectives at the top level.
- Divide the sub-objectives into tasks of appropriate size.
- Prioritize your tasks.
- Schedule your tasks.
- Complete the tasks.
- Track progress through indicators.
- Adjust the schedule and priorities according to progress.

This process will ensure that you focus on the right things and schedule them to happen, regardless of your goals.

If you don't want to set yourself a timetable but want to proceed at a more leisurely pace, you can still use the above approach in an adapted way. Instead of adding timeframes to goals and tasks, you can use their order of priority to guide implementation.

For example, you can put tasks into three categories: *pending*, *in progress*, and *finished*. The most important tasks can wait to be completed until you start working on them. When you promote specific tasks, you can move them to the Implementation category. And when you're done with them, you can move them to the Ready category. This way, you always have new tasks available, you know what's in the works and what you've already done, and this approach doesn't put the same time pressure on you as the previous process.

You have now reached the end of the book's third part, and you are well-equipped to start making your dreams come true.

Closing words

Delivering your vision is both a great and challenging skill. Too much, too fast, can easily lead to burnout and giving up, while too little will not help you stay in the growth zone to make real progress. By now, you've probably already identified areas in yourself where development is needed and others where you're already strong. This book was divided into three main sections, the first two of which were acronyms or shorthand. The first part was the FROM ZERO and focused on building the foundations for self-development. In it, we went through the essential things that contribute to and enable you to achieve success in a planned way:

- **Sleep** well.

- **Think** fast.

- Move and eat your way to energy.

- Create the economic conditions.

- **Ever** more advanced you.

- **The reason** for coping.

- Recognize the facts.

- Put things in order.

In this first part, the order of implementation did not matter so much, as all the things are helpful throughout the process of the second part. You can return to these chapters again and again depending on the challenges you experience with your own goals and self-development. The principles will help you think about and choose what is worth pursuing. And you will have learned by now that you have enormous power to make things happen, and if you spend your time on the wrong things, you will not reach your optimum potential. Which things covered in the FROM ZERO part were most important to you? Write down your main lessons here:

The book's second part focused on the acronym TO HUNDRED, which gave you a six-step action plan to meet your chosen goals. In this part, the order of the chapters is essential, as one step leads to another:

- ♦ Plan your way to success.

- ♦ Start where you are.

- ♦ Do enough of the right things.

- ♦ Assess progress and development.

- ♦ Progress towards the goal and enjoy the journey.

- ♦ **Reset** and move on to new adventures.

What goals did you choose to achieve, and what did you plan for? Write down below the main lessons you learned from this part:

And the last, or third, part of the book focuses on the timing of objectives. The book has chosen a timeframe of six months because too short may not allow you to achieve significant things, and too long a timescale risks getting lost along the way and not getting there. Of course, you don't have to make your plan on a six-month timeline; you can use any timeframe that suits your plan. You can also implement yourself without the pressure of a schedule, as Part 3 showed.

It's challenging to make a set of guidelines for specific goals because each of us comes from a different background and has a different motivation to get results. However, three different and practical example programs are included at the end of the book. They include:

- Developing your behavior.
- Fitness program inspired by Navy Seals.
- Writing a book.

The first of these programs focus on increasing your mental capacity. This program is simple but challenging. The second program focuses on developing physical skills based on the instructions of elite soldiers. And the third program gives an example of how to make a concrete product, a book. The purpose of the programs is not only to give you ready-made programs that you can start following but also to show you how to develop your own programs that will lead you to your goals.

There are usually two very challenging stages in writing a book: starting and finishing it. For this book, starting was very easy because the idea that you and I can create the best possible version of ourselves makes my keyboard buzz. By the time I write these closing words, I have already pruned out over 200 pages of good advice to make the book as practical and inspiring as possible. So, it's time for the final story, which shows that any of us can achieve any result, no matter where we come from, if we care enough and work hard enough to make it happen.

One day, some students went out to celebrate in the evening. They knew there was an exam the next day, but they decided it wasn't worth taking it anyway because they hadn't studied enough. So, the students went to the party and agreed that one of them would call the teacher in the morning and tell her that their car had a flat tire on the way and they could not get to the exam on time. And that's what happened. The teacher said all three students would be allowed to retake the exam the following week. So, the students studied hard for a week and were ready to take the exam at the scheduled time. However, the teacher said they would have to take the test in different rooms, which the students agreed to because they had all read well. However, when they took the exam, they noticed that there were only two questions:

- ♦ What is your name?

- ♦ Which tire blew out on your car last week?

The name got 10 points on the exam, and the tire question got 90 points if it was the same as everyone else's. This taught them that we often only fool ourselves when we do things poorly. Bad work usually leaves a short trail. Life is all about being able to adapt to circumstances and be the best version of yourself and your life in any given situation. This is possible by growing your skills, talents, and guts.

Are you like a potato, an egg, or a coffee bean? Perhaps this is a difficult question, so walk into your kitchen and keep reading. Are you in your kitchen now (you would be one of the very few if you did this)? Now, get out the three pots. Put a gallon of water in each of them. Put them on the stove and turn it on for all three pots. Now, put a couple of potatoes in one of the pots. Put a couple of eggs in the second pot and add a tablespoon of coffee grounds to the third pot. Let all these simmer for 20 minutes. Pour the water from the pot of potatoes and eggs and put them on a plate. The coffee, in turn, can be strained into a cup. Now look at this slightly quirky meal and wonder what you see. Sure, you still see a couple of potatoes, eggs and a cup of coffee. Now, try these with your finger. How do the potatoes feel? Very soft. How do the eggs feel? Very hard. How does coffee feel? Very wet. So, what happened? All three went through the same ordeal. The initially hard potato could not withstand the hot water environment and softened and crumbled. On the other hand, the chicken egg was very fragile before this ordeal but came out hard as a rock. On the other hand, coffee went into the hot pot dry and bitter and came out tasty and usable.

Who do you choose to be?

May the Lord bless you and keep you on your chosen path, for it has been said, *"Man plans his way, but the Lord guides his steps."*-Proverbs 16:9.

Reading recommendations and sources

Business Process Management Capabilities: A Scientific Edition by Dr Janne Ohtonen, https://www.amazon.co.uk/Business-Process-Management-Capabilities-Scientific/dp/B01K90YR86/

Marry Your Customers! Customer Experience Management in Telecommunications by Dr Janne Ohtonen, https://www.amazon.co.uk/Marry-Your-Customers-Experience-Telecommunications-ebook/dp/B078Q8Z7RL/

The 5-Star Customer Experience: Three Secrets to Providing Phenomenal Customer Service by Dr Janne Ohtonen, https://www.amazon.co.uk/5-Star-Customer-Experience-Providing-Phenomenal/dp/1524653659/

You Think You Are Doing Well? Become a Winner with Customer-Centric Process Leadership! by Dr Janne Ohtonen, https://www.amazon.co.uk/You-Think-Doing-Well-Customer-Centric/dp/952680550X/

Brainhack: Tips and Tricks to Unleash Your Brain's Full Potential by Neil Pavitt, https://www.amazon.co.uk/Brainhack-Tricks-Unleash-Brains-Potential/dp/0857086421

Why We Sleep: The New Science of Sleep and Dreams by Matthew Walker, https://www.amazon.co.uk/Why-We-Sleep-Science-Dreams/dp/0141983760/

Awaken the Giant Within: How to Take Immediate Control of Your Mental, Emotional, Physical and Financial Life by Anthony Robbins, https://www.amazon.co.uk/Awaken-Giant-Within-Immediate-Emotional/dp/0743409388

Unshakeable: Your Guide to Financial Freedom by Anthony Robbins, https://www.amazon.co.uk/Unshakeable-Your-Guide-Financial-Freedom/dp/1471164934

Money Master the Game: 7 Simple Steps to Financial Freedom by Anthony Robbins, https://www.amazon.co.uk/Money-Master-Game-Financial-Freedom/dp/1471148610

Can't Hurt Me: Master Your Mind and Defy the Odds by David Goggins, https://www.amazon.co.uk/Cant-Hurt-Me-Master-Your/dp/1544512279/

Man's Search for Meaning: The classic tribute to hope from the Holocaust by Viktor E. Frankl, https://www.amazon.co.uk/Mans-Search-Meaning-classic-Holocaust/dp/1844132390

S.U.M.O (Shut Up, Move On): The Straight-Talking Guide to Succeeding in Life by Paul McGee, https://www.amazon.co.uk/S-U-M-Shut-Move-Straight-Talking-Succeeding/dp/0857086227

Duckworth, A.L., Peterson, C., Matthews, M.D., & Kelly, D.R. (2007). Grit: Perseverance and passion for long-term goals. Journal of Personality and Social Psychology, 9, 1087-1101

Atomic Habits: The life-changing million-copy bestseller by James Clear, https://www.amazon.co.uk/Atomic-Habits-Proven-Build-Break/dp/1847941834

Brian Tracy, Goals! How to Get Everything You Want -- Faster Than You Ever Thought Possible, https://www.amazon.co.uk/Goals-Everything-Faster-Thought-Possible/dp/1605094110

Born to Win: Find Your Success by Zig Ziglar, https://www.amazon.co.uk/Born-Win-Find-Your-Success/dp/1613398336/

The Attention Economy: Understanding the New Currency of Business by Thomas H. Davenport, https://www.amazon.co.uk/Attention-Economy-Understanding-Currency-Business/dp/157851441X

The Procrastination Equation: How to Stop Putting Things Off and Start Getting Stuff Done by Piers Steel, https://www.amazon.co.uk/Procrastination-Equation-Putting-Things-Getting/dp/0273767704

ANNEX: Example programs

ow it is time to roll up your sleeves and develop your mind, body and brain. These three example programs are based on the latest research and practical experience in self-development. The first program focuses on developing your behaviors. Developing our behavior is very challenging and worth striving for because the better we can be for each other, the better off we will all be in this world.

The second program is based on a fitness program inspired by elite soldiers. This program allows you to train your body to the level required for the entrance exams. This program can also inspire you to join the popular CrossFit hobby, which involves similar exercises.

The final example is writing a book. The program is designed for beginning writers and focuses mainly on non-fiction writing.

Of course, you can adapt all the example programs to suit your goals and starting point. Get started today and have fun!

Developing your behavior

Developing your behavior is very challenging and worth striving for. The better we can be for each other, the better off we will all be. For those who are believers, Jesus-like behaviors are highly desirable. Of course, not everyone subscribes to this idea or wants to be better people. But that doesn't stop those of us who understand the value of improving our behavior, both for ourselves and for others. There are many benefits to improving our behavior:

- Improved self-esteem.

- The development of social relationships.

- Increasing goodwill.

- Improved quality of life for yourself and those around you.

- Achieving challenging things (which is what developing your behavior is) builds resilience, self-discipline, willpower, and the ability to achieve other challenging goals.

- Reinforcing good habits and eliminating bad ones.

Behavioral development is challenging, and developing a program that allows anyone to develop without knowing their situation does not make it any easier. But the good news is, I've been using the approach outlined here to build my behavior for years and have seen direct benefits in my professional and personal life. Of course, this work is never done, but there is always room to evolve as a person. Nor should this be done for the wrong reasons. It's not about being good enough as it is. It's more about the fact that self-improvement in all areas, including behavior, brings good feelings and improves one's own life and the lives of others. We pursue these things for our benefit and the benefit of others because we can.

The main content of the program consists of focusing on one behavior per week. We start by taking stock of your current situation and defining your goals. Then, you can develop your behavior in one topic per week. Finally, we will assess where you are after this, how you developed, and what you can do next. The behaviors you develop can either be negative ones you want to eliminate or positive ones you want to reinforce. It's entirely your choice which behaviors you want to put on your list, although this book gives you a sample list to start from. The idea is that you focus all your energy on that behavior each week and develop your thinking and actions around it. In this program, you choose a maximum of 12 topics to develop. This will be a 6-month program with 2 cycles (1 topic per week, 12 weeks, or 6 months). Of course, you could also choose 24 behaviors to develop for each week, but this approach runs a high risk of being too superficial, as, with each round of this program, you will deepen your development in each of the 12 areas. Either way, you have 24 topics to choose from, and you can either take half of them and do two rounds or go through them all.

Here are the seven steps we take in this program:

1. Setting goals and choosing behaviors.

2. Mapping the baseline situation.

3. Behavior development for 3 months.

4. Mapping the intermediate situation and re-selecting behavioral patterns.

5. Behavior development over the next 3 months.

6. Mapping the end state.

7. Lessons learned and next steps.

Let's start with the first step.

Step 1. Setting goals and choosing behaviors

Let's start with what you want to achieve with the program. In the space below, write in free text why you want to improve your behavior:

Consider whether the reasons you describe above are so desirable to you that you are willing to think about them every day for at least the next three months. If your answer is no, consider your reasons again and your underlying desires.

Next, think about what you want to develop and why. Below is a suggested list of essential behaviors that you can use as a basis for your list:

- Gratitude
- A positive attitude
- Calmness/patience
- Righteousness
- Kindness
- Respect
- Physical Fitness
- Mental Fitness
- Catching up
- Decisiveness
- Perseverance
- Cleanliness
- Economy
- Efficiency
- Forgiveness
- Hospitality
- Adoption
- Honesty

- ◆ Coherence

- ◆ Praying

- ◆ Humility

- ◆ Optimism

- ◆ Solution-oriented

- ◆ Sociability

- ◆ Sustainability

Now write in the space below which 12 you choose and why they are essential to you:

1.

2.

3.

4.

5.

6.

7.

8.

9.

10

11.

12.

The third step is to plan how you will improve your behavior. Write your commitments in the space below:

Your plan may include the instructions for this program, plus whatever else you feel you need to do to succeed.

Step 2. Identifying the initial situation

Now that you have chosen either of the 12 behaviors to focus on for the next few weeks, we can take stock of your current situation. First, fill in the list below with your choices and then rate your current situation on a scale of 0 to 10. 0 means you are beginning to practice the behavior, and 10 means you are already quite a master. If you like, you can also ask your friends to rate you for a more objective result.

Behavior model	Your perception of performance on a scale of 0-10	The performance given to you by a friend on a scale of 0-10

Now that you know the behaviors and where to start developing them, we can plan how best to develop them over the next three months.

Step 3. Developing behavior over three months

Now that you have 12 things to focus on, you can break down each behavior into three critical areas for development. In practice, you can think about the three most important things you should develop about that behavior. It is impossible to give a set of guidelines for this, so I recommend you take a piece of paper and a pencil and list everything you need to develop for each behavior, then choose the three most important ones.

Then, write down the behavior model and the three most essential things in the table below. Put one for Monday-Tuesday, one for Wednesday-Thursday, and one for Friday-Saturday. This way, you focus on one thing for two days. On Sunday, take a break from the program and review the week. How did it go? Which areas did you improve the most? Where do you still have work to do? Save the information in the Sunday column because if you do another round, you can use the information to develop your plan.

| | Development topic | | | Review by |
Behavior model	**Mon-Tue**	**Wed-Thu**	**Fri-Sat**	**Sun**
Week 1.				
Week 2.				
Week 3.				
Week 4.				
Week 5.				
Week 6.				
Week 7.				
Week 8.				
Week 9.				
Week 10.				

Week 11.

Week 12.

The table above should show one behavior pattern and its three most important things. You are ready to start the actual work! Start the following Monday and keep a diary of your thoughts and progress. Remember, you can spend as much or as little time as you like, and the only one you are cheating is yourself.

Step 4. Taking stock of the interim situation and re-selecting behavioral patterns

Congratulations, 12 weeks went by like wings? Now, it's time for a mid-term review. Complete the table below like before (don't look at your previous numbers until you've completed the table with your current situation).

Behavioral model	Current performance on a scale of 0-10	The performance given to you by a friend on a scale of 0-10	Change to the initial situation

In the Change column, fill in the change since the start status. Which behaviors have evolved and which have not? And have you perhaps taken a step back for some? Also, compare this with your diary for the last 12 weeks to gain further insights. I hope you have followed the process so far and found it helpful. Now, you can decide whether to continue with a new round of these (or change your) behaviors.

Step 5: Develop behavioral patterns over the next three months

Re-evaluate the development points for each behavior. Do you want to keep the same ones or perhaps change some of them to ones that work better for you? Fill the table below with the new information.

Development topic	Review by

Behavioral model	Mon-Tue	Wed-Thu	Fri-Sat	Sun
Week 13.				
Week 14.				
Week 15.				
Week 16.				
Week 17.				
Week 18.				
Week 19.				
Week 20.				
Week 21.				
Week 22.				
Week 23.				
Week 24.				

That way, you're ready for the next round, and sure, you already know what you're doing. Good luck!

Step 6. Mapping the end-state

Congratulations, you have another three months of behavioral development behind you. That's an outstanding achievement, and you've undoubtedly seen the benefits of this program in action by now.

So, let's see where you are now. As in previous rounds, fill in the table below with the behaviors you have chosen and the change of the prior assessment round:

Behavioral model	Your perception of performance on a scale of 0-10	Performance was given to you by a friend on a scale of 0-10	Change to the intermediate situation

What does it look like? Which areas have you improved in, and which have you not? What does your diary say about this, and how does it help you understand the results?

Step 7. Lessons learned and next steps

Congratulations on completing the behavior development program. Self-development is a noble pursuit that benefits both you and others. You can now gather your learnings and thoughts about the program and its impact and use them to decide your next steps.

First, consider why you started the program and what you wanted to achieve. Write here how the program has helped you to achieve your goals:

What was the most tangible benefit you got from the program and why?

Where are you with your behaviors today, and what (if anything) would you like to do next to improve them?

This brings us to the end of a six-month behavioral development program. How you use the knowledge and experience and what you do next is your choice. Whatever it is, I'm proud of you because not all people spend this much time developing themselves for their pleasure and the joy of others. I hope to see you soon!

Elite soldiers' fitness program adapted for us

Most of those who hear about the elite soldiers' fitness program quickly turn to the next page. I belonged to this camp myself, still traumatized by my military experiences in my youth. There, exercise was compulsory and largely unpleasant. However, I saw a series on YouTube about America's elite Navy Seals and their extremely demanding entrance exam, which includes Hell Week[*] . During that week, the candidates are subjected to extreme physical and mental stress, while both their diet and sleep intake are severely restricted (in practice, they sleep about 4-8 hours during the week). I certainly don't imagine I could survive such a week, but the idea of pushing myself in such a demanding way is intriguing... would I be up for it? So, I started researching the fitness requirements for the entrance exam alone and how much training I would need to do. I read everything I could get my hands on and watched all the Navy Seals-related videos I could find online. Finally, I contacted Mark Divine, who runs SealFit gym in California. He is a genuine Navy Seal, a tough Carpathian in experience and fitness. Now that he's retired from the military, he runs fitness programs for regular folks like you and me.

Putting a fitness program in a book is tricky because everyone starts from a different baseline. Maybe you're already in good shape and could pass the fitness test immediately. Or perhaps you're an office worker, like me, and your fitness level is low, even if you don't necessarily look it. Or maybe you've put on more live weight than you need to. Either way, each of us starts where we are, but we may also end up at the level of fitness required for the Navy Seals fitness test. And that's the goal of this fitness program. Why would you even want to accomplish that goal? That's up to you to decide. For me, it was about beating myself, exceeding my expectations, and making sure that at least getting into Navy Seals didn't depend on the fitness test (although it could depend on a thousand other things, starting with the fact that I'm too old and I'm not an American citizen and I don't want to kill anyone). But it

---

[*] https://www.youtube.com/watch?v=HR_zvFuvkEc

doesn't matter how realistic it would be to get there; it's more about a physical and mental victory for myself. I hope you'll join me on the journey! Potential benefits of this fitness program for you include:

- Develop your overall fitness and endurance.

- Increase your self-esteem by going beyond what you thought was possible.

- Diversify your training.

- Start a new hobby.

- Be prepared for tasks and situations that require physical and mental fitness.

- Know that if *Uncle Sam* calls you from the States and asks you to take the Navy Seals fitness test, you'll pass!

Before we get down to the nitty-gritty of what the fitness test should be, do this fitness test for yourself first and then see how close you are. Allow about an hour and a half in total for the test. Warm up first, at least 10-15 minutes before starting the test. Also, be careful if you are not used to doing these movements (in that case, I recommend watching YouTube instructional videos to learn and practice the correct technique before even attempting the test). It's not worth breaking yourself, and even in Navy Seals, there will be an automatic medical disqualification if you break yourself. So it would be best if you didn't do it as part of this program.

Below is a table where you can record your results. It also lists the movements and breaks allowed. After this table, I will tell you how to do each movement, and then you can take the test.

Date of fitness test: _______________________________

Test topic	My performance	How did it feel?
As many push-ups as you can do in 2 minutes		
10-minute break	--	
As many abdominal muscle movements as you can manage in 2 minutes		
10-minute break	--	
As many chin-ups as you can do at once		
10-minute break	--	
500 m swimming or 2 km rowing		
10-minute break	--	
2,5 km run		

These are simple moves in principle, but they are relatively easy to cheat (for example, by making incomplete moves) and are not allowed.

Therefore, here are instructions on how to perform each move acceptably.

Push-ups:

- Start in a high plank position, arms and legs straight.

- In the down position, the chest should touch the ground.

- In the upright position, the arms and legs should be completely straight.

- Pelvis straight all the time, no swaying

- Knees must not touch the ground.

Abdominal muscle movements:

- Hands crossed and touching shoulders and elbows on sides.

- In the upright position, elbows should touch the knees.

- In the low position, the back and head should contact the ground.

Chin up:

- In the starting position, hang straight.

- In the up position, the chin should be above the bar, and the whole body should be straight in the down position.

- No extra movements on the legs or hips to facilitate getting up.

Swimming:

- The swimming style is the Combat Sidestroke (see YouTube videos on how to do it). This is not the typical swimming style taught in swimming schools.

Rowing:

- If you can't do the swim, you can do the 2km row instead (if you were actually in the Navy Seals test, there would be no option).

I recommend you try all the movements before you start the fitness test and ensure you are doing them with the correct technique. As with everything else in this book, you're only fooling yourself, so you better do them correctly. When you're done, do the test and record your results in the table above before you continue reading this.

What results did you get? And how close do you think you are to passing the Navy Seals fitness test? Below are the minimum required scores as well as the recommended scores. You will not pass the test if you do not meet the minimum score in all areas. And suppose you want to get into Navy Seals. In that case, you should get at least the recommended scores because if enough candidates pass the test (as is usually the case), those who score below the recommended scores will be dropped.

Test topic	Minimum requirement	Recommended performance
As many push-ups as you can do in 2 minutes	50	90
As many abdominal muscle movements as you can manage in 2 minutes	50	85
As many chin-ups as you can do at once	10	18
500 m swimming or 2 km rowing	12 minutes 30 seconds	9 minutes

| 2,5 km run | 10 minutes 30 seconds | 9 minutes 30 seconds |

How close did you get? Congratulations anyway! Now you know where you stand, and you have targets to beat. Now that you know your starting point, we can start the two-month fitness program.

This is not a mindless muscle-building program, but we are developing our physical and mental fitness. The goal is not just to get through this but to come out the other end stronger and better. This fitness program will not require one outstanding sporting performance but hundreds of challenging exercises that will develop you holistically step by step. So, stay focused and on schedule, and give yourself the gift to make your body like a tuned-up fighting machine and sharp as a knife's edge! How do you best prepare for these fitness sessions?

- Use your breathing technique to give your muscles and brain the needed oxygen. Concentrate on your breathing even outside of exercise. Use the so-called 4x4 technique, where you inhale for 4 seconds, hold your breath for 4 seconds, exhale for 4 seconds, and hold your breath again for 4 seconds. Repeat this breathing technique for at least 5 minutes before you exercise to oxygenate your body, be ready for work, and calm your mind to focus.

- Talk only positive things to yourself. What you say and think about yourself directly affects your performance. So tell yourself that you can do what you need to and have what it takes to do it already within yourself. I brag to myself *every day and get stronger and stronger every day*. Of course, you can make up your phrase to motivate you to keep going.

- Visualize yourself doing the exercises and making progress. Top athletes use the technique to their advantage, whatever their sport, so it's good for you too. It builds new connections in your brain and prepares your body to do what it needs to do. For example, scientific studies show that people who visualize themselves playing the piano learn to play it significantly faster than those who start without visualization.

- Set milestones that you want to achieve and bring you the joy of success. Big goals can be broken down into smaller goals (for example, in a marathon, focus on the next kilometer instead of the whole distance).*

- Eat and drink healthily. Your body needs proper nutrition, so eat plenty of vegetables, greens, and protein. It would be best to have good carbohydrates for energy, for example, from wholegrain products. Cut out the sweets, sodas, juices, and sweets, focus on healthy eating, and you'll see the effects directly in your body composition.

It isn't easy to show in the book how each movement should be done, and there are often different versions of the movements. Therefore, I recommend that whenever you are not sure how to do a move correctly, find it on YouTube and watch the instructional video on how to do the move. Then, practice the move technique to get it right before you do the fitness routine for the day. This will ensure you get the maximum benefit from the movements and don't break yourself with the wrong technique. All the movements in this program are commonly used in fitness and can be easily found online, including in English.

Week 1.

Monday

Instructions:

- Leg squat[†] : Stand with good posture and a tight core. Feet are about shoulder-width apart, and toes may point slightly outward. Squat backward while raising your arms in front of you. Drop your hips back to about a 90-degree angle. Remember to keep your back straight at all stages of the squat, including the bottom. Also, remember to check that

---

* Don't worry, with this fitness program you don't have to run a marathon!
† https://youtu.be/4VbfkpqXmDw

your knee and toe stay in line with each other with every movement (if you don't keep these aligned, you will quickly get sports injuries).

- Butterfly belly* : Lie on your back on the floor. Keep your stomach tight. Bring the soles of your feet together (your knees rise off the ground to the sides). Bring your arms straight over your head and crunch yourself up with your abdominal muscles. At the same time, bring your arms from above to the front, using your abdominal muscles to crunch yourself up. At the end of the movement, touch your hands to the slippers. Finally, descend in a controlled manner with your back rounded and your abdominal muscles braking (simultaneously, bring your arms straight over your head). Be careful not to bend your knees too much (beyond your toes when looking down).

Warm-up:

- Do 3 rounds: run 200 meters, do 10 leg squats without weight, 10 rounds of forward arm rotation, and 10 rounds of backward arm rotation.

Strength training:

- Do 5 rounds and 5 repetitions of each round: leg squat, weight on shoulders (lightweight).

Fitness training:

- 500 yards of running or rowing.

- 40 leg squats without weight.

- 30 species of butterflies.

- 20 push-ups.

- 10 chin-ups. If you can't pull these many chins, help yourself by jumping to get started and then do a slow descent. Take a short break in between if necessary.

Refrigeration:

- Stretch, especially the hips and shoulders.

- Drink water, and eat protein within half an hour of finishing your workout.

Tuesday

Instructions:

---

* https://youtu.be/HghGGudXuGM

- Mountaineer[*] : Get into a push-up position with your fingers pointing straight ahead. Elbows point backward. Keep your core tight and your neck as an extension of your back. Then, jump forward alternately, with one foot on the ground and the other coming forward.

- General movement[†] : Stand up straight in a shoulder-width position and squat down so that your palms touch the floor at the front of your body. Push backward with your feet so that your hands remain on the floor, and you end up in a push-up position; from there, drop your chest to the floor by folding your arms. Push yourself up off the floor and back into a squat position with your feet as quickly as possible. Jump up from the squat with a bang and try to bounce as high as possible.

Warm-up:

- 200 yards.

- 40 mountaineering movements, 20 on each foot.

- 200 yards.

- 20 push-ups.

Fitness training:

- Do 3 rounds of 400m run, 10 general movements (burpee), 10 leg squats with lightweight, 10 reps with knees to elbows hanging from the bar (like a chin-up, but instead you pull the knees to the elbows and return down).

Cooling:

- Stretch.

- Drink water, and eat protein within half an hour of finishing your workout.

Wednesday

Warm-up:

- 400 yards.

- 5 rounds: 10 leg squats without weight, 5 push-ups, 5 abdominal muscle movements.

Strength training:

---

[*] https://youtu.be/eeACppfwDlY
[†] https://youtu.be/v3wT0LqeD0s

- ◆ Do 5 rounds and 5 reps in each round: leg squat, weight on chest (lightweight).

Fitness training:

- ◆ Do as many rounds as possible in 10 minutes: 5 chin-ups, 5 push-ups, 10 leg squats with your weight on your chest.

Refrigeration:

- ◆ Stretch.

- ◆ Drink water and eat protein within half an hour of finishing your workout.

Thursday

Warm-up:

- ◆ 20 minutes of free-choice movements and repetitions: push-ups, abdominals, leg squats, chin-ups, general movements, etc.

Resilience training:

- ◆ 10 minutes of running, swimming, or rowing as fast as possible.

Refrigeration:

- ◆ Stretch.

- ◆ Drink water, and eat protein within half an hour of finishing your workout.

Friday

Warm-up:

- ◆ 3 rounds: 150 m rowing, 10 leg squats without weight, 10 leg squats with weight on chest.

Strength training:

- ◆ Do 5 rounds and 5 repetitions of each round: leg squat with weight on head.

Fitness training:

- ◆ 10 rounds, so that the number of repetitions per movement is reduced from 10 to one per round: leg squat with weight on the head, climbing stairs or box with both feet, abdominal muscle movement.

Cooling:

- ◆ Stretch.

- Drink water, and eat protein within half an hour of finishing your workout.

Week 2.

Congratulations! The first week is behind us, and it's time to continue the program in the second week.

Monday

Warm-up:

- First 30, then 20, and finally 10 repetitions of each movement: crotch jump, leg squat, rotation of both arms.

Strength training:

- Do 5 rounds and 5 reps in each round: lifting a barbell from the chest to the head (lightweight).

Fitness training:

- 1 km rowing or swimming.

- 25 lifting a bar weight from the chest to the head with an appropriate weight.

- 20 chin-ups.

Refrigeration:

- Stretch, drink water, and eat protein within half an hour of finishing your workout.

Tuesday

Instructions:

- Step squat * : Keep your body in good posture throughout the movement. Step forward so that your front knee rests on the ground at a 90-degree angle and your back thigh goes horizontal. Then push up.

Warm-up:

- Run 500 yards.

- Do 3 rounds: 5 repetitions per leg of step squats, 10 push ups, 15 abdominal muscle movements.

---

* https://youtu.be/z9z-uZwglNY

Fitness training:

- Do as many laps as possible in 20 minutes: 25 yards of step squats forward, 10 general movements, 25 yards of jogging back to the starting position.

Cooling:

- Stretch, drink water, and eat protein within half an hour of finishing your workout.

Wednesday

Warm-up:

- Do 3 rounds: 200 m run, 5 vertical push-ups on the bar, 5 lunges.

Strength training:

- Do 5 rounds and 5 reps in each round: lifting a barbell from the chest to the head (lightweight).

Fitness training:

- 4 rounds: 400 m run, 10 vertical push-ups on the bar, 10 weighted ball throws on the ground.

Refrigeration:

- Stretch, drink water, and eat protein within half an hour of finishing your workout.

Thursday

Warm-up:

- 20 minutes of free-choice movements and repetitions: push-ups, abdominals, leg squats, chin-ups, general movements, etc.

Fitness training:

- 15 minutes of running, swimming, or rowing as fast as possible.

Refrigeration:

- Stretch.
- Drink water, and eat protein within half an hour of finishing your workout.

Friday

Warm-up:

- 250 yards of marshland.

- 15 push-ups.

- 250 yards of marshland.

- 15 vertical push-ups with a bar.

Fitness training:

- First do 21 reps, then 15, and then 9 reps: mountain climbers, vertical push-ups on the bar, abdominal muscle movements.

Cooling:

- Stretch, drink water, and eat protein within half an hour of finishing your workout.

Week 3.

Congratulations! The second week is behind us, and it's time to continue the program in the third week. By now, you should be starting to see clear improvements in your fitness.

Monday

Warm-up:

- 400 yards.

- First 10, then 8, 6, 4, and 2 reps: leg squats, jumping chin-ups (so you assist by jumping).

Strength training:

- Do 5 rounds and 5 repetitions of each round: a push-off with the appropriate weight.

Fitness training:

- 5 rounds: deadlift with heavy weight, 6 vertical push-ups with bar, 9 general movements.

Refrigeration:

- Stretch, drink water, and eat protein within half an hour of finishing your workout.

Tuesday

Instructions:

- Front squat vertical push-up[*]

Warm-up:

- 3 rounds: 200 m run, 25 lunges, 15 abdominal muscle movements, 5 push-ups with your hands off the floor at the bottom.

Fitness training:

- Do as many laps as possible in 20 minutes: 400 m run, 10 front squat push-ups with a barbell, 10 knees to elbows with a chin-up bar.

Cooling:

- Stretch, drink water, and eat protein within half an hour of finishing your workout.

Wednesday

Help:

- Pull up

- Dip[†]: Keeping your arms straight either on the dip rack or the rings, lower your torso, fold your arms to a 90-degree angle, and push yourself back to the starting position.

Warm-up:

- 500 yards of swamp.

- 3 rounds: 10 cross-country, 10 mountain climbers, 10 vertical push-ups to a slight squat.

Strength training:

- Do 5 rounds and 5 repetitions in each round: a combination of a sumo lift and a vertical lunge.

Fitness training:

- 500 yards of swamp.

- 25 a combination of a sumo lift and a vertical lunge.

- 25 weight balls thrown against the wall.

- 25 extension cords.

- 500 yards of swamp.

---

[*] https://youtu.be/7LawTfuici0
[†] https://youtu.be/gh2aDkzHpkI

Cooling:

- Stretch, drink water, and eat protein within half an hour of finishing your workout.

Thursday

Warm-up:

- 20 minutes of free-choice movements and repetitions: push-ups, abdominals, leg squats, chin-ups, general movements, etc.

Fitness training:

- 20 minutes of running, swimming, or rowing as fast as possible.

Cooling:

- Stretch, drink water, and eat protein within half an hour of finishing your workout.

Friday

Warm-up:

- 10 sandbag lifts from the ground to the right shoulder.
- 400 yards.
- 10 sandbag lifts from the ground to the left shoulder.

Strength training:

- Do 5 rounds and 5 reps in each round: Olympic-style weightlifting from the ground up.

Fitness training:

- 5 rounds: 10 Olympic-style deadlifts from the ground, 100 m run, one minute break.

Refrigeration:

- Stretch, drink water, and eat protein within half an hour of finishing your workout.

Week 4.

Monday

Instructions:

- White squat*

Warm-up:

- 3 rounds: 200 m run, 10 squats, 10 push-ups.

- Rotation of the shoulders.

Strength training:

- Do 5 rounds and 5 repetitions of each round: squat.

Fitness training:

- 5 laps: 400 m run, 15 squats.

Cooling:

- Stretch, drink water, and eat protein within half an hour of finishing your workout.

Tuesday

Instructions:

- Back support on the bench[†].

Warm-up:

- Lift the sandbag off the ground on each shoulder alternately for 10 minutes.

Fitness training:

- First 15, then 12, 9, 6, and 3 reps of each movement per round: kettlebell lunge, box jump, bench press.

Refrigeration:

- Stretch, drink water, and eat protein within half an hour of finishing your workout.

Wednesday

Warm-up:

- 400 yards.

- 3 rounds: 5 leg squats, 5 jumping squats, 5 push-ups, 5 abdominal movements.

---

* https://youtu.be/9ReLVXceyhg
† https://youtu.be/GEDW6rzQPys

Strength training:

- ◆ Do 5 rounds and 5 repetitions of each round: leg squat with weight on shoulders.

Fitness training:

- ◆ 100 chin-ups.

- ◆ 100 push-ups.

- ◆ 100 abdominal muscle movements.

- ◆ 100 leg squats without weight.

Refrigeration:

- ◆ Stretch, drink water, and eat protein within half an hour of finishing your workout.

Thursday

Warm-up:

- ◆ 20 minutes of free-choice movements and repetitions: push-ups, abdominals, leg squats, chin-ups, general movements, etc.

Fitness training:

- ◆ 25 minutes of running, swimming, or rowing as fast as possible.

Cooling:

- ◆ Stretch, drink water, and eat protein within half an hour of finishing your workout.

Friday

Warm-up:

- ◆ 250 yards of rowing.

- ◆ 15 vertical push-ups.

- ◆ 250 yards of marshland.

- ◆ 15 jumping on a box.

Strength training:

- ◆ Do 5 rounds and 5 repetitions of each round: vertical push-up with the appropriate weight.

Fitness training:

- 3 rounds: one minute of throwing a weighted ball on the wall, one minute of a combination of a sumo pole vault and a vertical jump, one minute of jumping on a box, one minute of vertical push-ups on the bar, one minute of full rowing, one minute of rest.

Refrigeration:

- Stretch, drink water, and eat protein within half an hour of finishing your workout.

Week 5.

We are now halfway through the program. If the previous exercises seemed easy, we now switch gears and increase the challenge.

Monday

Warm-up:

- Stretch.
- 400 yards.
- 10 leg squats.

Strength training:

- Do 5 rounds and 5 repetitions of each round: leg squat with appropriate weight.

Resilience training:

- 50 leg squats with lightweight.
- Climbing 100 boxes with a lightweight.
- Walk 800 yards with as heavy a backpack or weight as possible.

Fitness training:

- 30 Olympic-style cross-country races up.
- 20 chin-ups.
- 20 Olympic-style cross-country races up.
- 10 chin-ups.
- 10 Olympic-style cross-country races up.
- 5 chin-ups.

Resilience training:

- 5 km run.

- 3 rounds: 20 abdominal muscle movements with weight.

- 20 spinal muscle movements.

Cooling:

- Stretch, drink water, and eat protein within half an hour of finishing your workout.

Tuesday

Instructions:

- Abdominal muscle movement with leg lift[*] : Lie on your back on the floor. Lift your feet 5 cm off the ground. Lift one leg 30 cm off the ground alternately.

- Lumbosacral movement with arms swinging to the sides[†] : Lie on the floor on your stomach. Put your arms straight out in front of you. Lift arms and legs off the ground. Swing your arms straight out in front of you to your sides to close your sides and back.

Warm-up:

- Stretch.

- 400 yards.

- 10 vertical push-ups with a bar (lightweight).

Strength training:

- Do 5 rounds and 5 reps in each round: vertical push-up with bar.

Resilience training:

- 4 rounds: 20 vertical push-ups on the bar with lightweight, 5 chin-ups with extra weight, 100 m run with weight.

Fitness training:

- 15 rounds: 1 crunch from the ground, 5 leg squats with weight on shoulders, 30-second break.

Resilience training:

- 15 laps: 30 seconds of full rowing, 30-second break.

---

[*] https://youtu.be/iIdD4nzdFpw
[†] https://youtu.be/-3ngqJtQ0Bo

- ♦ 100 abdominal muscle movements with leg lifts.

- ♦ 100 back muscle movements, swinging the arms to the sides.

Refrigeration:

- ♦ Stretch, drink water, and eat protein within half an hour of finishing your workout.

Wednesday

Warm-up:

- ♦ 20 minutes of free-choice movements and repetitions: push-ups, abdominals, leg squats, chin-ups, general movements, etc.

Fitness training:

- ♦ Run, swim, or row for as long and fast as possible.

Refrigeration:

- ♦ Stretch, drink water, and eat protein within half an hour of finishing your workout.

Thursday

Warm-up:

- ♦ Stretch.

- ♦ Run 400 yards.

- ♦ 10 cross-country driving with lightweight.

Strength training:

- ♦ Do 5 rounds and 5 repetitions of each round: ground strokes.

Resilience training:

- ♦ 50 cross-country trains with lightweight.

- ♦ 75 moorland traction with lightweight.

- ♦ A 400-metre walk with as heavy a weight as possible.

Fitness training:

- ♦ First 50 reps, then 35, and finally 20 reps: throwing the ball on the wall, chin-up, double jumps.

Resilience training:

- ♦ 3 km run.

- The longest possible plank.

- Sitting against a wall for as long as possible.

Refrigeration:

- Stretch, drink water, and eat protein within half an hour of finishing your workout.

Friday

Warm-up:

- Stretch.

- 800 yards.

- 10 bench presses (lightweight).

Strength training:

- Do 5 rounds and 5 reps in each round: bench press.

Resilience training:

- 5 rounds: 15 bench presses, 20 one-arm bench presses with a dumbbell, 50 m walking squat with weight on head and arms straight.

Fitness training:

- 15 rounds: 1 crunch from the ground, 5 leg squats with weight on shoulders, 30-second break.

Resilience training:

- 3 laps: 500 m rowing, 400 m running, one minute break.

- 50 knees to elbows with a chin-up bar.

Cooling:

- Stretch, drink water, and eat protein within half an hour of finishing your workout.

Saturday

Warm-up:

- Stretch.

- 400 yards.

- 5 rounds: 5 chin-ups, 10 push-ups, 15 leg squats.

Fitness training:

- 4 laps: 800 m run, 40 chin-ups, 70 push-ups.

Resilience training:

- 30 minutes of running with a weighted backpack on your back.

Refrigeration:

- Stretch, drink water, and eat protein within half an hour of finishing your workout.

Week 6.

Monday

Instructions:

- Frog shops[*]

Warm-up:

- Stretch.

- 500 metres of swamp.

- 2 frog movements with a light bar weight.

- 10 leg squats with weight on shoulders.

Strength training:

- Do 5 rounds and 10 leg squats with weight on shoulders.

Resilience training:

- 4 rounds: 20 leg squats with weight on shoulders, 25 jumping squats, 50 m walk with as much weight as possible.

Fitness training:

- 5 rounds: 5 frog movements, 10 general movements.

Resilience training:

- 7 km run.

- 100 abdominal muscle movements.

---

[*] Frog Complex, https://youtu.be/X9x5WgQly7U

- ♦ 100 abdominal muscle movements with leg lifts.

Cooling:

- ♦ Stretch, drink water, and eat protein within half an hour of finishing your workout.

Tuesday

Warm-up:

- ♦ Stretch.

- ♦ 500 yards of swamp.

- ♦ 10 bench presses with lightweight.

Strength training:

- ♦ Do 5 rounds of 10 reps of bench press.

Resilience training:

- ♦ 50 bench presses with a lighter weight.

- ♦ Walk 800 yards with as much weight as possible.

Fitness training:

- ♦ 5 rounds: 5 frog movements, 10 general movements.

Resilience training:

- ♦ 2 km run with extra weight.

- ♦ 10 rounds: 10 chin-ups, 20 push-ups, 30 leg squats.

- ♦ 2 km run with extra weight.

Cooling:

- ♦ Stretch, drink water, and eat protein within half an hour of finishing your workout.

Wednesday

Warm-up:

- ♦ 20 minutes of free-choice movements and repetitions: push-ups, abdominals, leg squats, chin-ups, general movements, etc.

Fitness training:

- ♦ Run, swim, or row for as long and fast as possible.

Refrigeration:

- Stretch, drink water, and eat protein within half an hour of finishing your workout.

Thursday

Warm-up:

- Stretch.

- 800 yards.

- 10 cross-country driving with lightweight.

Strength training:

- Do 5 rounds of 10 repetitions of the groundstroke with the appropriate weight.

Resilience training:

- 5 rounds: 15 cross-country with lighter weight, 20 box jumps, 50 meters of four-legged walking (i.e., all limbs on the ground).

Fitness training:

- 15 Olympic-style cross-country races up.

- 200 yards.

- 20 Olympic-style cross-country races up.

- 400 yards.

- 30 Olympic-style cross-country races up.

- 800 yards.

Resilience training:

- 5 km of rowing.

- 100 abdominal muscle movements on the bench.

Cooling:

- Stretch, drink water, and eat protein within half an hour of finishing your workout.

Friday

Warm-up:

- Stretch.

- 500 yards of swamp.

- 10 bench presses with lightweight.

Strength training:

- Do 5 rounds of 10 repetitions of bench presses with the appropriate weight.

Resilience training:

- 50 bench presses with a lighter weight.
- 75 push-ups.
- 400 yards walk.

Fitness training:

- Do as many as you can in 20 minutes: 250 yards rowing, 15 squats alongside a pull-up on the bar.

Resilience training:

- 800 m long run and break.
- 400 m sprint and break.
- 200 m sprint and break.
- 100 m sprint and break.

Refrigeration:

- Stretch, drink water, and eat protein within half an hour of finishing your workout.

Saturday

Warm-up:

- Stretch.
- 10 with a sandbag to get up off the ground.

Fitness training:

- 800 yards.
- 10 rounds: 10 crunches from the ground, 10 push-ups, 10 abdominal muscle movements, 10 leg squats.
- 800 yards.

Resilience training:

- 30-minute run.
- 100 abdominal muscle movements by swinging your legs in the air.

- ♦ 100 feet of swinging back and forth in the air up and down while lying on the ground.

Refrigeration:

- ♦ Stretch, drink water, and eat protein within half an hour of finishing your workout.

Week 7.

Monday

Warm-up:

- ♦ Stretch.

- ♦ 800 yards.

- ♦ 5 leg squats with lightweight on shoulders.

Strength training:

- ♦ Do 5 rounds of 10 repetitions of leg squats with appropriate weight on the shoulders.

Resilience training:

- ♦ 5 rounds: 15 leg squats with lighter weight on shoulders, 25 mountain climbers, hang from the bar as long as you can.

Fitness training:

- ♦ 3 rounds: 20 Olympic-style upward push-ups, 15 raw lifts from the ground, 10 chin-ups, 10 general movements.

Resilience training:

- ♦ 3 rounds: row at full speed for one minute, rest for one minute.

- ♦ 100 abdominal muscle movements by swinging your legs slightly off the ground.

- ♦ 100 feet of swinging back and forth in the air up and down while lying on the ground.

Cooling:

- ♦ Stretch, drink water, and eat protein within half an hour of finishing your workout.

Tuesday

Warm-up:

- Stretch.

- 500 yards.

- 5 bench presses.

Strength training:

- Do 5 rounds of 10 repetitions of bench presses with the appropriate weight.

Resilience training:

- 50 bench presses with a lighter weight.

- 100 jump chin-ups.

- Walk 800 yards with as much weight as possible.

Fitness training:

- 3 minutes each at full speed, one minute break in between rowing, leg squat, weight on the head, throwing a weighted ball on the ground, abdominal exercises, 800 m run.

Resilience training:

- 3 km run.

- 3 rounds: 10 knees to elbows, chin-up with bar, 10 back muscle movements.

Cooling:

- Stretch, drink water, and eat protein within half an hour of finishing your workout.

Wednesday

Warm-up:

- 20 minutes of free-choice movements and repetitions: push-ups, abdominals, leg squats, chin-ups, general movements, etc.

Fitness training:

- Run, swim, or row for as long and fast as possible.

Cooling:

- Stretch, drink water, and eat protein within half an hour of finishing your workout.

Thursday

Warm-up:

- Stretch.
- 800 yards.
- 5 cross-country driving with lightweight.

Strength training:

- Do 5 rounds of 10 repetitions of the groundstroke with the appropriate weight.

Resilience training:

- 4 rounds: 50 lunges with a lighter weight, 10 box jumps, hang from the chin bar chin over the bar as long as you can.

Fitness training:

- 5 laps: as many push-ups as possible, 400 yards run.

Resilience training:

- 10 laps of the 50-yard sprint.
- 100 abdominal muscle movements.
- 100 back muscle movements where you move your arms from front to side.

Refrigeration:

- Stretch, drink water, and eat protein within half an hour of finishing your workout.

Friday

Warm-up:

- Stretch.
- 500 yards of swamp.
- 5 bench presses.

Strength training:

- Do 5 rounds of 10 bench press repetitions with the appropriate weight.

Resilience training:

- 50 bench presses with a lighter weight.
- A 400-meter walk with as much weight as possible.

Fitness training:

- 10, 9, 8... 4, 3, 2, 1 repetition per round: chin-up, abdominal, back muscle.

Resilience training:

- 5 km run.

- The longest possible plank.

- Sitting against the wall for as long as possible with your feet hooked.

Refrigeration:

- Stretch, drink water, and eat protein within half an hour of finishing your workout.

Saturday

Warm-up:

- Stretch.

- 800 yards.

- 15 with a sandbag to get up off the ground.

Fitness training:

- 8 rounds of 30 seconds of each movement at full speed: rowing, push-ups, jumping jacks.

Resilience training:

- 30-minute run.

Cooling:

- Stretch, drink water, and eat protein within half an hour of finishing your workout.

Week 8.

Another month of training is ending, so let's give it another week.

Monday

Warm-up:

- Stretch.

- 800 yards.

- 5 leg squats with lightweight on shoulders.

Strength training:

- Do 5 rounds of 10 repetitions of leg squats with the appropriate weight on your shoulders.

Resilience training:

- 50 leg squats with a lighter weight on the neck.

- Walk 800 yards with as much weight as possible.

Fitness training:

- First 40 reps, then 30, 20, and 10 reps in each round: Olympic-style push-up, knees to elbows, chin-up with bar.

Resilience training:

- 7 km run.

Refrigeration:

- Stretch, drink water, and eat protein within half an hour of finishing your workout.

Tuesday

Warm-up:

- Stretch.

- 400 yards.

- 5 bench presses.

Strength training:

- Do 5 rounds of 10 bench press repetitions with the appropriate weight.

Resilience training:

- 5 rounds: 15 bench presses with lighter weight, 20 one-handed push-ups, 50 m walk with weight.

Fitness training:

- 3 rounds with a weighted line: 500 m rowing, 20 box jumps, 15 chin-ups.

Resilience training:

- 2 rounds of the 800 m sprint.

- 100 feet swinging up and down in the air while lying on your back.

- 100 from the back muscle by swinging the arms from front to side and back.

Refrigeration:

- Stretch, drink water, and eat protein within half an hour of finishing your workout.

Wednesday

Warm-up:

- 20 minutes of free-choice movements and repetitions: push-ups, abdominals, leg squats, chin-ups, general movements, etc.

Fitness training:

- Run, swim, or row for as long and fast as possible.

Refrigeration:

- Stretch, drink water, and eat protein within half an hour of finishing your workout.

Thursday

Warm-up:

- Stretch.

- 500 yards of swamp.

Strength training:

- Do 5 rounds of 10 repetitions of the groundstroke with the appropriate weight.

Resilience training:

- 50 with a lighter weight.

- 75 sumo pastures.

- A 400-metre walk with a weight.

Fitness training:

- 2 km run.

- 30 general movements.

- 2 km run.

Resilience training:

- 2 km of rowing.

Refrigeration:

- Stretch, drink water, and eat protein within half an hour of finishing your workout.

Friday

Warm-up:

- Stretch.

- 800 yards.

- 5 bench presses.

Strength training:

- Do 5 rounds of 10 repetitions of bench presses with the appropriate weight.

Resilience training:

- 4 rounds: 20 bench presses with lighter weight, 20 push-ups, and a 25 m squat walk with weight on the bar.

Fitness training:

- As many rounds as possible in 15 minutes: 5 leg squats, 30 weight throw on the wall.

Resilience training:

- 6 laps of the 200 m sprint.

- 100 feet swinging up and down in the air while lying on your back.

- 100 from the back, swinging the arms from front to sides and back.

Cooling:

- Stretch, drink water, and eat protein within half an hour of finishing your workout.

Saturday

Warm-up:

- Stretch.

- 3 rounds: 200 m run, 10 weighted ball throws on the wall, 10 jumping jacks, 10 abdominal movements.

Fitness training:

- 3 km run.

- ♦   10 rounds: 5 chin-ups, 10 push-ups, 15 leg squats.
- ♦   2 km run.

Resilience training:

- ♦   30 minutes of running with extra weight.

Refrigeration:

- ♦   Stretch, drink water, and eat protein within half an hour of finishing your workout.

Week 9.

Congratulations! You've been beating yourself up for two months now, and it's undoubtedly showing in your results. So, let's return to the elite soldier fitness test with which we started this fitness program. See how you get on it now:

Date of fitness test: _______________________________

Test topic	My performance	How did it feel?
As many push-ups as you can do in 2 minutes		
10-minute break	--	
As many abdominal muscle movements as you can manage in 2 minutes		
10-minute break	--	

As many chin-ups as you can do at once	
10-minute break	--
500 m swimming or 2 km rowing	
10-minute break	--
2,5 km run	

Compare your results with the previous round. What happened? I bet you smashed all your expectations while gaining significantly more muscle and improving your fitness.

If you need more challenges, see how long it takes you to complete each of these challenges:

- 1,000 chin-ups
- 1,000 abdominal muscle movements
- 1,000 push-ups
- 1 000 general movements
- 10 km run
- Half marathon (21 km run)

The results are printed on my wall to break my records at least once a year. This keeps the motivation up and shows that I can do these things; it's just a matter of how fast! Good luck with your fitness goals; I know you can exceed all your expectations.

Writing a book

Writing a book is a dream for many. I published my first non-fiction book in 201; this is my sixth since then. The Finnish Society of Information Writers has already supported two of my books, and companies have supported others. At one time, the paperless office was predicted as the death of books, but neither has yet come close to materializing. According to Statistics Finland, Finland has been publishing literature since the 17th century, and today 13 000-14 000 titles are published in Finland every year[*] . Thus, there is still a strong production and demand for books in Finland. A book is a great way to get your ideas on paper (or now on screen) and for others to use. For example, Pastor Jukka Norvanto has published more than 60 Christian books, widely regarded as Finland's best source for Bible study. In doing so, he has been a blessing to hundreds of thousands of Finns. Of course, there are many other similar examples in Finland, where one book has changed the lives of thousands. This program of examples will focus exclusively on the book's writing, especially on the early stages of the process. Later stages, such as finishing the book, finding a publisher, and publishing it, are not included this time.

One of the most common concerns among beginning (and even experienced) writers is that they may not have enough interesting things to say or don't know the subject until they write a book. These concerns arise out of fear, and by the time you read this book, I'm sure you'll already agree with me that we don't do things out of fear but out of a deep-seated desire to add value to our lives and the lives of others. If you are interested in sharing your thoughts through a written output (which can also be a blog or other way of sharing your thoughts), please continue through this writing program and then evaluate at the end if writing a book is for you. As for the concerns I mentioned earlier, it usually ends up the other way around, and you have too many ideas and information and must prune them. In writing, as in speaking, it is

---

[*] https://www.stat.fi/tup/suomi90/huhtikuu.html

much harder to say a lot in a little than a little in a lot. So, your challenge will not be that you don't have enough to say but how best to write it.

The mere desire to write a book proves you can do it. You probably already have a topic or a range of issues in mind that you would like to write about if you decide to write a book. This program is a designed (and proven) way to map out your ideas and plan your book. You can use it to outline your book and write it. And remember, the plans are made so that you can assess whether the plan is worth implementing before spending more time on it. If you feel you don't want to be a writer at the end of the plan, it's better to abandon the idea early than to waste any more time on it. However, I think you will find the opposite happens, and you will end up writing at least something (I published over 200 blog posts and won a prize for them before I wrote my first book by following the advice shared here).

The most common concerns and antidotes to writing books are:

- ◆ You must be born with a gold pen in your hand.
  - ▪ Not at all. Writing is a skill like reading, running, or anything else. My mother tongue average was about 7 grades in school, and in the matriculation exams, I got such a bad grade in my mother tongue that I don't even remember it anymore. However, I have published 6 books with well over 50,000 readers and over 200 blog posts with over 200,000 readers. So, you, too, can acquire the skill, if you wish.

- ◆ You must write millions of words to become a writer.
  - ▪ Not at all. Books can contain as many or as few words as the book needs. For example, the shortest Harry Potter (J.K. Rowling) book contains 77 325 words, and the most extended 198 227. However, Charlie and the Chocolate Factory (Roald Dahl) contains only 30 644 words. Of course, if you want to go entirely to the other

extreme, Tolstoy's War and Peace has 587 287 words. So, your book can be any length you like.

- You need inspiration or enlightenment to write a book.

  - Not at all. Of course, if you get one, your writing may be easier at times. But very few writers have written an entire book in an inspired state. Writing, like other things in life, takes work; sometimes, it's more accessible and sometimes more complex. Most importantly, you progress one step at a time and don't give up.

- If you start writing, the text will come naturally.

  - Not at all. The keyboard doesn't tap, and the pen doesn't scribble words on paper as it flutters in the wind. A good plan will help ensure you get there. For example, I started with a six-page table of contents for this book. This then turned into 150 pages of notes on the possible contents of the book. I wrote the first words in the actual book file only after this. The actual writing was, therefore, much easier, as I spent months just preparing for the writing.

- The book must be perfect.

  - Not at all. As they say, beauty is in the eye of the beholder. Your book may not be rubbish, but the Yanks, for example, have proved with their flat-earth and anti-vaccine clubs that there is a demand for everything somewhere. You can do a lot to improve your book, such as asking others to review the content and hiring a professional proofreader. And a book is never finished, as there is always something that could be improved in every book.

♦ Writing a book is difficult.

■ Not at all. Of course, there are more accessible and more challenging moments in writing. Sometimes, the text comes in a torrent; sometimes, the tap is closed. Sometimes, there are clear thoughts, hazy ones. That's why it's best to plan your book as well as possible before you write it: it helps you move forward regardless of your state of mind.

It would be best to know what you want to achieve and why it is important to you when writing a book, as with all your other goals in life. There will inevitably come times in writing a book when you don't feel like doing it anymore (writing this book has taken me a significant amount of time, too). These are the times when you need to stick to the habits that support your writing (write at least 50 words a day because you'll probably end up writing more anyway, but don't push yourself beyond that). It would be best to remind yourself why writing a book is essential to you. It helps you keep going and pick up a keyboard (or a pen if you still have one). So, start planning your book around why you want to write it and what your readers will get from it. This book program focuses on non-fiction, as I haven't written any fiction yet, so I couldn't give you any valid advice. However, these guidelines have been used to publish over 1,000 pages of non-fiction in six books, so you're off to a good start if you want to write non-fiction.

The most important and exciting topics for you are:

The topics you know most about:

Who you want to write to (target audience):

The most important and exciting topics for your target audience are:

The information above will help you identify the areas where your interests and those of your target audience meet. This will give you a list of topics on which you could write a book.

All the subjects you could write a book about:

The book you want to write:

The aim of your book is:

> *What a reader would say about your book when they read it:*

> *What kind of review would a reader write about your book after reading it:*

The questions above aim to outline what added value the book would bring to the reader. This will help to shape the content of the book in the future. It will also help you understand why you want to write the book:

> *You want to write a book because:*

The more inspiring and specific your answers to the questions above are, the better start you will make with your book plan. Of course, you need to consider your and your reader's motivations beyond just the questions above, but these will get you off to a good start. I usually write a short description of the book at this stage and outline the text on the back cover that tells you what the book is about. The final back cover text will only take shape when the book is finished, but it will serve as a red thread for you about the book's contents at this stage.

Take, for example, a book you could write about selling (all the examples in this program are made up for practical reasons). The answers to the previous questions could be:

- The most important and exciting topics for you are.

  - Talking to people, the latest cars, and motorbikes, making the most of work, watching YouTube videos, walking the dog, playing golf

- The topics you know most about.

  - Selling cars, talking to people

- Who you want to write to (target audience)

  - For other salespeople

- The most important and exciting topics for your target audience are.

  - Increasing sales, closing deals, attracting customers, getting the best price, looking good to the boss, pleasing customers, and knowing the products you sell.

- All the topics you could write a book about

  - Selling cars, selling in general, selling motorcycles, playing golf with friends, best videos on YouTube, outdoor activities

- The book you want to write.

  - On sales, focusing mainly on car sales.

- The aim of your book is to

  - Helping other car dealers sell cars ethically and efficiently.

- What a reader would say about your book when reading it

  - These are some excellent tips; I could try these things myself; that's a good tip on how to talk to people. I didn't know you could present cars like that.

- What kind of review would a reader write about your book after reading it?

  - This is the best car sales book I have read because it gave me practical advice on how to increase sales ethically and sustainably. It keeps customers coming back for more.

- You want to write this book because:

  - I know all the tricks of the trade when it comes to selling cars, and I can teach them to other salespeople without having to cheat or mislead their customers. In this way, I can feel that I have helped my colleagues do their jobs better, thus increasing customer satisfaction in the car sales industry. This will also help buyers because they will receive a good and ethical service that will change their perception of the car trade in the long run. This is part of my legacy for present and future generations.

Of course, all the examples above would be very different if you had written them. If anything, it also proves that you have a unique contribution to this world. This also makes each book different and of high quality in its way.

By now, you should know the book and what you want to achieve with it. So, the next step is to consider suitable titles for your book. At this stage, the title of your book may not be final, but it will help you focus on the right content during the planning phase. For example, the title of this book, *Zero to One Hundred,* was born out of the book's aim to help readers reach their goals no matter where they start (and the assumption was that most readers would be starting their goals very early). The second part of the title, *Six Months,* was a later addition for psychological reasons. As we discussed earlier, goals that are too short or too long-term cause problems, so six months is a psychologically workable time frame. That's how I came up with *Zero to Hundred in Six Months.*

So, what is a good book title? One that immediately grabs the reader's attention. People first look at the front cover, back cover, and the table of contents. Some may also flick through the book's pages and see what it looks like. And usually, the decision to buy is made by then. Unfortunately, 80% of the books bought are never read, which is a shame, but from the point of view of the book's name, this is irrelevant. There are whole books written about book titles and cover design, so I won't go into the details of that, but will focus on the main guidelines for you:

- Keep the name short; surprise with a name.

- Make several versions of the name and test these with your target audience; they can help you shape the final name.

- Make the title of the book as descriptive of the content as possible; don't gimmick too much or give the wrong impression of what the book is about.

- Use the subtitles to describe the book's content in more detail.

- Keep the book title easy to read and understand; don't use complicated words.

- Make the name as easy to remember as possible.

Now, you can sketch out titles for your book.

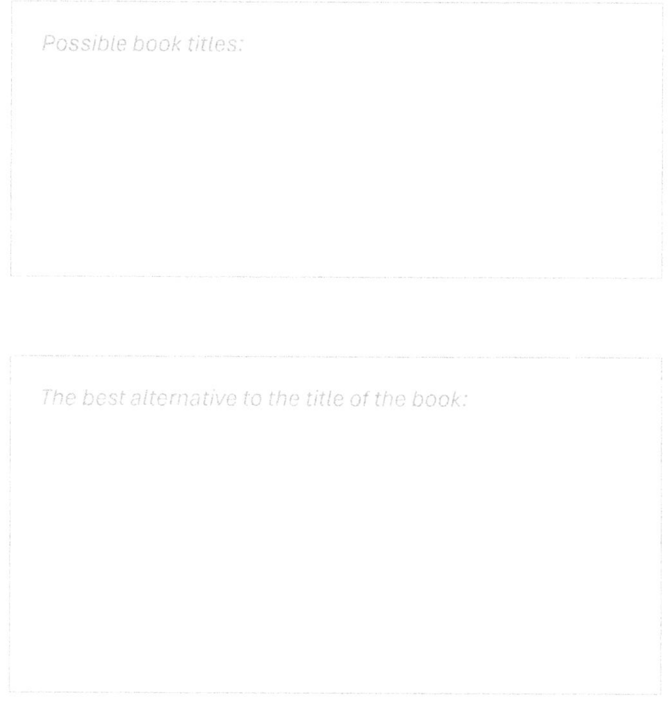

Use these questions to evaluate the title of your book:

- Is the title descriptive and clear?

- Does the headline grab the reader's attention?

- Does the title offer clear benefits to the reader?

- Do readers know what the book is about?

- Is the title of the book still in line with your and your reader's objectives as described earlier?

Now you have your book's topic area and title outlined, we can move on to planning the content of your book. So, we return to the target audience you defined earlier and their needs.

What are your target audience's main challenges in your chosen subject area? List as many as you can:

From the list above, what are the five most important challenges for your target audience:

From the list above, which is the most critical challenge for your target audience?

What do they need to meet this challenge? List as many solutions as you can:

Now you know both the problems of your target audience and the best solutions. If your list feels light or you want to improve its quality, I recommend doing more online research. Search and watch videos on the topic, and read what others have written. Usually, at this stage, I get hold of all the books on my chosen subject. For example, for Zero to 100, I read through over 200 books. This helps me to understand what has already been said on the subject, the most common problems, and the solutions to them. It also helps to find gaps that others have either missed entirely or have only skimmed through.

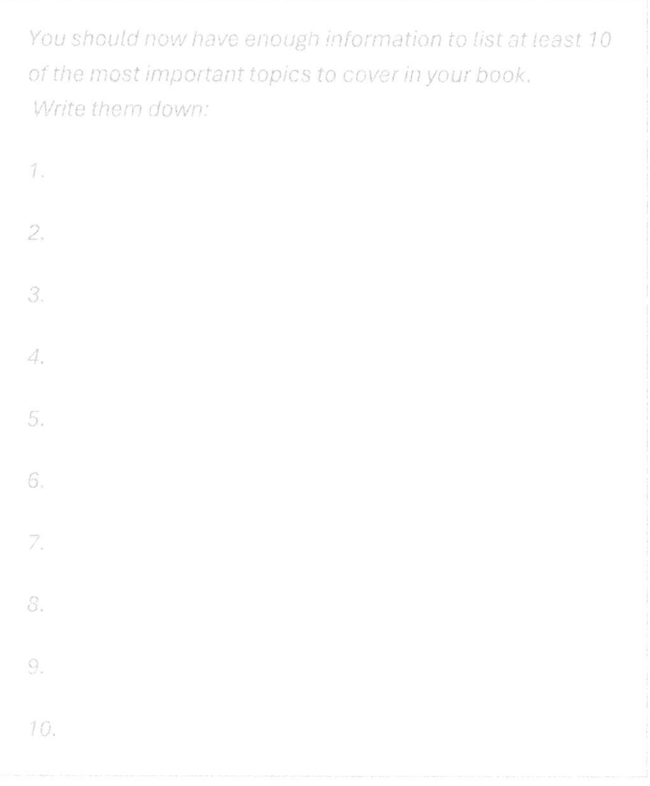

Let's go back to our earlier sales book example and use the technique above to design that book. Let's imagine we came up with the title of the book "Double your car sales - guaranteed!" and thus the 15 topics the book could contain:

1. What is car sales?

2. The importance of car sales for the economic success of society

3. Career opportunities in car sales

4. Earning potential in car sales

5. Developing your sales skills

6. Sales management

7. Selling additional products

8. Sales challenges

9. Sales prizes

10. Steps to becoming a star salesman

11. Other career options

12. History of sales

13. Learning product features

14. Leveraging technology in car sales

15. History of car sales

You can come up with more than 15, but in that case, you should prioritize the content to get a list of the 15 most important topics. You can rank the issues even higher and select the 10 most important issues. So, make a list of the 10 most important issues, or main content, for your book in the order you want:

1.

2.

3.

4.

5.

6.

7.

8.

9.

10.

If we continue from the previous example, the ten chapters of a car sales book could be:

1.   What is car sales?

2.   Career opportunities in car sales

3.   Earning potential in car sales

4.   Steps to becoming a star salesman

5.   Developing your sales skills

6.   Sales challenges

7.   Sales prizes

8.   Learning product features

9. Selling additional products

10. Leveraging technology in car sales

If you were doing the exercise, your content list would look different. Even if we could both write a book on the subject, readers would still get added value because we would give them different advice. In the example above, the general sales-related chapters were omitted to focus better on the book's content in the title, i.e., car sales. Of course, it's also worth noting that you don't have to have precisely 10 chapters to think about; this is just a good average. For example, the Zero to 100 book ended up with more chapters because I decided to convert the title to an acronym (which made determining the content much more challenging). I would have had even more advice to give, but it would not have fit into the book's structure. You have the same artistic freedom to define the content of your book.

You now have a plan for the book's target audience, added value, title, and main content. It's time to start planning the individual chapters, which are ten in this example and the bottom. We'll break each chapter into smaller chunks to add value and make it easier to write the content. So, use this same approach for all the leading figures you have.

Fill in the base below for all the leading content figures. First, enter the title of the main chapter and then the 18 sub-entries. For example, if the chapter is about sales skills, the sub-content chapters could include conversation skills, influencing skills, car skills, and so on. Use the same approach for the content chapter as you used earlier for the main chapter, i.e., list at least 18 main topics (of course, you can list more if possible).

Main content:

Now, you have a list of subtopics for one main chapter. Next, select the 10 most essential topics from the list above and put them in a logical order. You will then have the top ten most important topics for the chapter.

Now, you have the sub-content figures planned for one main chapter. You can repeat the exercise for all the leading figures before moving on to the next step. This will give you a first overview of what your book could contain. If you follow the sample numbers given here, you should now have 10 main content numbers and 10 sub-content numbers under each. So, you have a list of 100 essential things to write about in your book! You're probably no longer worried about not having enough to say in your book. You should have a slightly different number of headings and subheadings to suit your book's topic, the title, and your knowledge of the subject.

The next step in the design process is to convert all the topics in the sub-content figures into claims. This will give you what is called a red thread to follow for each chapter. For example, if the main content chapter is Sales Skills and the sub-content chapter is Conversation Skills, convert this Conversation Skills into a strong argument. It could be, for example, *that conversational skills are vital to car sales success*. So now, please return to your baseline and turn it into a strong argument.

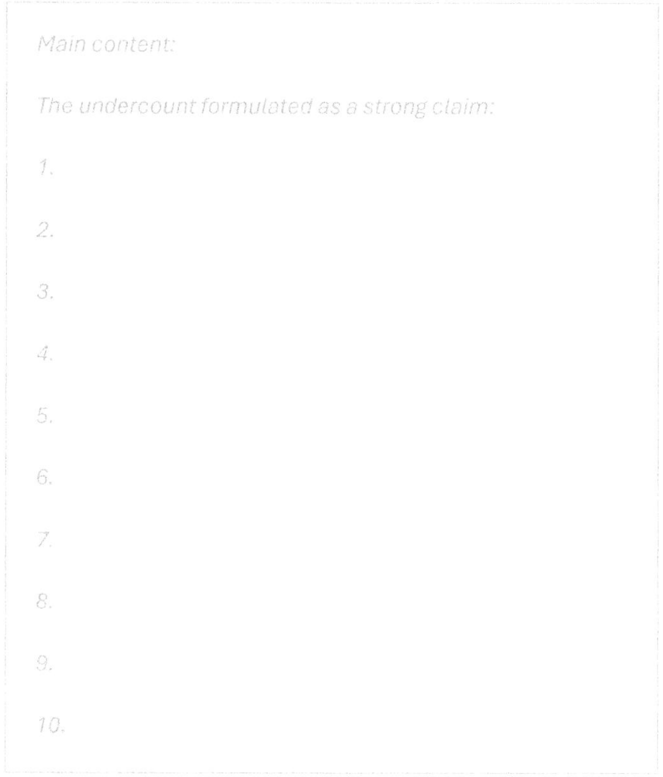

We go one level deeper into the content of the book. Next, consider the three most important things to do to make each claim a reality. For example, if the claim is that "*Creative, conversational skills are vital to car*

sales success," what are the three most important things to do to make this happen? They could be greeting people with a look in the eye and a firm handshake, caring about what the customer wants, and being prepared to discuss a wide range of issues. Of course, it could be something else. You know the most critical points in your area best and can add them to this list. The number doesn't have to be three; it can be any other number that suits the topic.

Main content:

The sub-content numbers and their main lessons:

1.
a.
b.
c.

2.

a.
b.
c.

3.

a.
b.
c.

4.

a.
b.
c.

5.

a.
b.
c.

6.

a.
b.
c.

7.

a.
b.
c.

8.

a.
b.
c.

9.

a.
b.
c.

10.

        a.

    b.

    c.

Once you've done this for all the sub-contents, you'll have 300 of the most essential pieces of advice about your book. This is more than enough material for a book. The program may seem over-simplified, but don't let that fool you. If you do your design work well, you will have a lot of valuable advice to give. And as mentioned earlier, this is not the book's final content but a starting point. The content is final only when you decide it is.

Now, you can start writing. It's easy to break this down into daily or weekly goals, where you write one paragraph at a time. This doesn't require you to write in a straightforward order; you can write the chapters in the order you want because you already have a clear plan. Sometimes, you may find as you write that things need to move to another chapter or you missed something important that you want to add. Sometimes, some content doesn't fit the book, and you may leave it out. So how much should you write in a day? This is entirely your choice. Many famous authors write very different amounts per day. Look at this list to see how many words famous authors have written in a day:

- Arthur Conan Doyle: 3 000

- Ernest Hemingway: 500

- Graham Greene: 500

- Lee Child: 1 800

- Mark Twain: 1 400

- Stephen King: 2 000

No matter how much you write, it's normal. Any word count greater than zero is acceptable. But there's no shortcut to happiness here; the book requires a writer - is that you?

Now is the time to decide. Given everything you know above, do you want to become a writer? If not, never mind, something more important is waiting. And if you want to be a writer, now, if ever, is an excellent time to commit to it:

Responsibility agreement for writing the book

Responsible person:

Responsibility partner:

The responsible person will do everything possible to write the book within this timeframe:

If the person responsible does not get the book written on time, the consequences are:

And this will be followed up:

Signatures

Signature of the responsible person:

Signature of the responsibility partner:

Place and time:

You have taken your first steps as a writer, so today is a good day to start writing your first 50 words. See you at the booksho

Dr Janne Ohtonen